CANADA AND THE
AMERICAN PRESENCE

COUNCIL ON FOREIGN RELATIONS BOOKS

Founded in 1921, the Council on Foreign Relations, Inc. is a non-profit and non-partisan organization of individuals devoted to the promotion of a better and wider understanding of international affairs through the free interchange of ideas. The membership of the Council, which numbers about 1,600, is made up of men and women throughout the United States elected by the Board of Directors on the basis of an estimate of their special interest, experience and involvement in international affairs and their standing in their own communities. The Council does not take any position on questions of foreign policy, and no person is authorized to speak for the Council on such matters. The Council has no affiliation with and receives no funding from any part of the United States government.

The Council conducts a meetings program to provide its members an opportunity to talk with invited guests who have special experience, expertise or involvement in international affairs, and conducts a studies program of research directed to political, economic and strategic problems related to United States foreign policy. Since 1922 the Council has published the quarterly journal, *Foreign Affairs*. From time to time the Council also publishes books and monographs which in the judgment of the Committee on Studies of the Council's Board of Directors are responsible treatments of significant international topics worthy of presentation to the public. The individual authors of articles in *Foreign Affairs* and of Council books and monographs are solely responsible for all statements of fact and expressions of opinion contained in them.

The members of the Board of Directors of the Council as of September 1, 1975, are: Robert O. Anderson, W. Michael Blumenthal, Zbigniew Brzezinski, Douglas Dillon, Hedley Donovan, Elizabeth Drew, George S. Franklin, Edward K. Hamilton, Gabriel Hauge (Treasurer), Nicholas deB. Katzenbach, Bayless Manning (ex officio), Harry C. McPherson, Jr., Alfred C. Neal, James A. Perkins, Peter G. Peterson, Lucian W. Pye, David Rockefeller (Chairman), Robert V. Roosa, Marshall D. Shulman, Cyrus R. Vance (Vice Chairman), Paul A. Volcker, Martha R. Wallace, Paul C. Warnke, Franklin Hall Williams and Carroll L. Wilson.

CANADA AND THE AMERICAN PRESENCE

The United States Interest
in an Independent Canada

John Sloan Dickey
President Emeritus

and

Bicentennial Professor of Public Affairs
Dartmouth College

Whitney H. Shepardson, Senior Visiting Fellow
(1971-1972)
Council on Foreign Relations, New York

A Council on Foreign Relations Book
Published by

New York University Press • *New York* • *1975*

Copyright © 1975 by Council on Foreign Relations, Inc.
Library of Congress Catalog Card Number: 75-10905
ISBN: 0-8147-1758-6

Library of Congress Cataloging in Publication Data

Dickey, John Sloan.
  Canada and the American presence.
  Includes bibliographical references and index.
  1. Canada—Relations (general) with the United
States. 2. United States—Relations (general) with
Canada. 3. Nationalism—Canada. 4. Canada—
Civilization—American influences. I. Title.
E183.8.C2D52   301.29'71'073   75-10905
ISBN 0-8147-1758-6

Manufactured in the United States of America

Contents

Introduction

Written by an American, this study aims primarily at greater American understanding as a requisite of wise policy in the U.S.-Canada relationship rather than the solution of specific problems.

It is well to acknowledge that, however much such a study relies on the work of countless others, there can be no pretense of describing in a full-bodied way the scope and the intricacy of this relationship. We are dealing with an ongoing interplay of vastness and intimacy—of similarities and differences, of the past and the present, of the public and the private—all gathered together in a drama of disparities and of alternating attraction and rejection that has no counterpart in the international community. In such an interplay where there is room for almost anything to be both true and untrue, the overall portrayal must be a considered judgment.

In presenting my judgment, I have made extensive use of Canadian sources, particularly in describing the American presence and Canadian nationalism's response to it. The understanding sought here can best be achieved by giving Americans some firsthand exposure to perhaps the most basic consideration of all: how concerned Canadians feel. And yet it must be emphasized that the judgment presented is that of an American observer, not a Canadian composite.

Any effort at understanding "how Canadians feel" must reckon with the fact that upward of 30 percent of all Canadians, indeed the oldest Canadians of all except for the Indians and the Eskimos, have had a significantly different Canadian experience, culturally and nationally, from all other Canadians. This fact, the French fact, has been a central aspect of Canadian national life for over two hundred years; more recently it has become a critical issue. Although Quebec separatism today is possibly less a threat to Canada's national cohesion than it seemed in the 1960s, the issue and its underlying concerns will surely continue to smolder in Canada's domestic affairs for the indefinite future.

Traumatic as this conflict has been for Canada internally, it has not so far been a major problem in the U.S.-Canada relationship. If, unhappily, at some future date separatism should prevail or become imminent, it would present problems for the relationship of the two nations that are beyond useful speculation here. It is entirely possible, of course, that as Canada moves further in the direction of realistic acceptance of the French fact in her national life as a counter to the appeals of separatism, there will be an increasingly important French-Canadian factor, per se, in her policy toward the United States as, indeed, is already the case with certain other nations, particularly the Francophone countries. In the main, however, these possibilities lie in the future.

For the particular purposes of this study, it is necessary to emphasize that French-Canadian nationalism is very different from the Canadian nationalism dealt with here. The former seeks to protect and strengthen the distinctive culture, especially the language, of French Canada; the primary threat to a prospering "French fact" is perceived as *les Anglais* of English Canada. In contradistinction, the Canadian nationalism examined here has been historically and today is mainly the sentiment of English-speaking Canada; its primary aim is to protect and strengthen Canada as an independent national society from the threat of what is perceived as "Ameri-canization."

Regardless of how the separatism issue develops the day may come when Quebec is more concerned about the American presence, but as matters stand today it is primarily concerned with getting the needed capital and technology for building a modern industrial society. It is not greatly concerned with where these necessities come from so long as they come on Quebec's terms, which, as will be seen hereafter, will not likely be as unwelcoming as Ottawa's in respect to foreign investment, nor as negative, for example, as Ontario's discouragement of competition from American securities dealers. Quebec does place great importance on the protection her society gets from the Anglo-Saxon sea surrounding her by the language barrier and a proudly distinctive cultural heritage. Any breaking of these dikes, e.g., by nonresident control of local publishing houses, is quickly repaired by provincial regulation. Such Quebec policy positions will be noted where relevant to the purpose of this study, but since this purpose excludes comprehensive treatment of the French fact and French-Canadian nationalism, it is well to assume that except where explicit reference is made to either French-Canadians or Quebec, statements herein may not be applicable to French Canada.

Western nations are now quite at ease in their domestic affairs with the concept of a "mixed society" where public policy, public programs, even public operation and ownership, meet private activity of every kind at the proverbial indivisible line of the "seamless web." This mix of the public and private has received less attention, however, in international relations. In part this reflects the fact that our thinking and terminology are still dominated by the concept of sovereign states as separate institutional entities whose dealings with each other across sharply defined international borders are governed by official foreign policies and the processes of diplomacy. This classical concept still corresponds to reality in many things in international affairs, but relations between two advanced societies today increasingly embrace a limitless flow of private activities and attitudes that shape and reshape the interface of the relationship.

The U.S.-Canadian experience is the most conspicuous example of this transcending, transnational, public-private mix. Above and beyond both diplomacy and national rhetoric this relationship has, in fact if not in theory, become an organic system of human affairs.

Inevitably, this relationship has its asymmetrical aspects. Most fundamentally, it is a fact that the cultural impact is largely within Canada, and correspondingly that it is *de minimis* and goes all but unnoticed in the United States. The intimacy of the relationship itself presents a problem for Canadian nationhood such as Americans have never known. It means that there is inevitably a more sustained, more personal nationhood concern by individual Canadians than could ever be true for the average American. This overarching disparity is one of the rare situations where Canada, so to speak, overwhelms the United States; in nearly all other situations capable of quantitative description the asymmetry "favors" the United States in ratios that are rarely, if ever, less than the ten to one in population, and usually the disparity is vastly greater —for example, defense expenditures are over thirty-five to one.

The uniquely pervasive private character of the relationship does, however, have special import for Americans. It means that good relations are more dependent upon the quality of private American understanding than in the case of any other United States international relationship, whether with friend or foe. Assuredly, these two nations are not immune either to official folly or to the beneficial influence of wise diplomacy. But the outsized impact of the American presence on Canadian life demands that better understanding on the part of Americans be raised from the low priority of a nice aspiration to at least par with official policy, as a decisive determinant of the relationship's health. There is no need to belabor the interdependence of public attitudes and wise policy in democratic societies, but it should be emphasized that this study's wide-lens view of policy is based on the premise that it will either be a many-splendored mix of public and private inputs, or it will be a very poor thing indeed.

It is legendary that Canadians are born knowing that "the United States will get you if you don't watch out" and that Americans die knowing nothing about Canada except that "it's cold up there". Such generalizations have less validity today than ever before, but they are the stuff of which problems are made, unless contained by mutual understanding.

Understanding has no more mortal enemy than a mistaken assumption. Whatever else Americans take for granted about their neighbor, nothing impedes better understanding more than the common American assumption that Canadians and Americans are alike, that the concerns of the two countries are similar, that they have a common view of history, and that Canada has nothing to fear from a well-intentioned United States. Of course, it is just because there is a large measure of truth in these assumptions that the untruth in them must be rigorously resisted by Americans as well as by Canadians who champion a distinctive Canadian nationhood.

And yet, Canadians overtly preoccupied with fear of an American take-over of their country tend to exaggerate the dangers of an intimacy from which geography and history permit no escape.

For over two decades now the tide of Canadian nationalism has been rising. It is more evident in certain regions, particularly Ontario, than in others and, of course, in Quebec it is crossed and diffused by the riptide of French-Canadian nationalism. But everywhere in Canada today the "new nationalism," the other side of the coin from the country's endemic regionalism, is a force to be reckoned with in both its positive and negative aspects. Americans may be helped in their understanding if they approach Canadian nationalism from two somewhat paradoxical premises: first, that despite the fact that Canada has over two hundred years of continuity as an evolving national society, much of her nationalism today has the self-conscious intensity of a newly created, somewhat uncertain, nation; second, that Canadian nationalism in its fundamental motivation is as old as the United States, in other words, that it is *inescapably* (and that is precisely the right word) a reaction to the American presence, past and current.

The central focus of the study is on what—perhaps after

Quebec separatism—is Canada's most fundamental concern, namely, independent nationhood in the face of a growing American presence in all sectors of Canadian life. Any special significance this study may have is not in the subject itself, which has been obsessively discussed by Canadians, but rather in an American effort to be more sensitive to the problem, and to understand better the United States national interest in a truly independent Canada.

Finally, a word of caution is advisable about any American approach to the subject of this study. Like French-Canadian separatism, Canadian nationalism and nationhood are not always easy subjects in the Canada-U.S. dialogue, a fact that manifests itself in various ways. On the one hand certain nationalists suspect, indeed almost resent, this kind of American interest in Canadian affairs as having ulterior motives, a form of neo-imperialism: "We don't want Americans to confer our independence on us." At the same time, Canadian nationalism often condemns the Canadian establishment in business, government, and the universities even more harshly than it does the United States. Naturally enough, this is not something many Canadians, particularly those who must deal regularly and responsibly with Americans, want taken too seriously. These difficulties are intrinsically instructive, but they do suggest a certain caution for Americans as they seek to understand today's Canadian nationalism: it is very close to the national nerve.

PART I

The Americanization Syndrome

CHAPTER 1

The Enduring Presence: Geography and History

Reality, not academic pedantry, raises geography and history to critical relevance in the U.S.-Canada relationship. In no other bilateral United States relationship are these two fundamentals so constantly entwined in the nation's foreign policy. Together they have created the asymmetries that dominate the relationship and thereby become the decisive forces to which policy must be responsive. The impact of this reality, however, has been and will continue to be far greater in Canada than in the United States.

Fisheries and furs, the early economic attractions of the northern sector of the continent, were not, as every schoolboy is supposed to know, activities that resulted in large, stable settlements. The northern climate and the ice-age heritage of a land dominated from the Atlantic to the western plains by the rocky surface of the Canadian Shield made for few agricultural opportunities. The physical fact of geography, plus the widening gap in population growth created large disparities of time and magnitude in the development of these two contiguous North American societies. Geographic differences were, of course, abetted by divergent political, economic, and social forces, but these forces were themselves dynamically shaped by the great natural variations of climate and opportunities for land use of the two countries.

Modern technology and transportation have modified the role of climate, distance, and topography, but lest geography as well as history be prematurely banished to the fashionable irrelevance of the past, it may be helpful to mention several fundamental aspects of United States-Canada relationship whose roots are grounded in geography rather than policy.

Most basic of all is the disparity in size of the two populations, the United States being about ten times larger than Canada's twenty-two million. This is the basic disparity from which most of the other disparities, many of them substantially larger, derive. Naturally enough, there are few comparisons, so to speak, that flow uphill against the steep difference in population size. Where there are exceptions, as, for example, the fact that Canadians on a per capita basis in 1971 had $4,476.19 of life insurance compared to $775.60 in the United States,[1] these are usually indications of certain inconspicuous but culturally significant differences in the two societies.

A second major configuration of the relationship that derives directly from geography and which is probably the most basic and enduring form of the American presence is the fact that 90 percent of all Canadians live within two hundred easy miles of the United States border, most of them, indeed, within an hour's drive or the flick of a TV switch. For better or worse—daily, directly, and inescapably—this American propinquity is the single most pervasive fact of Canadian national life. The people of no other major nation are similarly pinned to the border of a single neighboring country. To a degree never imagined when the vivid expression was introduced into international relations, Canadians are a border people.

The fact that the border operates very unequally as the dividing line between these two national cultures is, of course, a matter of history as well as geography. The fact is that the American presence in all forms floods downstream into Canadian life while the Canadian presence, except in trade statistics, is rarely perceptible south of the border.

However true it is that Canadian life is dominated to a high degree by its southern exposure, Americans do well to remember another geographic fact, namely, that the North, of which there is a lot in Canada, has long played a leading role in Canada's view of itself and is increasingly regarded both emotionàlly and materially as a distinctive Canadian characteristic in the relations of the two countries. The Canadian historian, Carl Berger, remarked that "from the days of the French explorers . . . to John Diefenbaker's invocation of the northern destiny of the nation, detached observers and patriotic spokesmen alike have fixed upon the northern character of Canada as one of the chief attributes of her nationality." For Canada the North was what the West was to the United States except, as Berger says, "Unlike the American frontier of free land . . . the north itself was inexhaustible." [2] At least so it seemed until recently. Today the competition for oil, gas, minerals, and water, along with the presence of aircraft of every sort, not to mention snowmobiles and the spreading threat of pollution, are rapidly bringing a sense of the exhaustible even to the vastness of the Canadian north. Along with such newfound attributes of national wealth and interest, the North is also increasingly invoked by Canadians as the ineradicable "Canadian fact" which, along with the "French fact," gives Canada a protective distinctiveness from the United States.

The North and the intercontinental missile have combined to make Canada a border country in quite another sense, namely, as the strategic "nuclear border" between the United States and the Soviet Union. It was this geographic circumstance that led in 1958 to the integration of the North American Air Defense Command of the United States and Canada (NORAD), an arrangement which has been the most official "continentalism" ever ventured in peacetime by the two nations.

Finally, mention should be made of the fact that Canadian nationhood and its nationalism must constantly come to terms with the nationwide regionalism that springs from and thrives on the geography of the country. Whether it be the historic, chronic economic shortfall of the Atlantic provinces, the dominating strength of Ontario, the idiosyncracies of prairie politics, the proud remoteness of British Columbia, or, above all, Quebec's historic individuality and separateness, any understanding of Canada and her policies must constantly reckon with the endemic regionalism that Canadian nationhood holds in uneasy embrace. This is but one area where Americans would do well not to mistake the appearance of similarity or similar terminology for the reality of similarity. American regionalism is a fact, but it is far from being the same thing in either form or function as its Canadian counterpart. In the United States, regionalism is itself divided and dispersed by fifty different state governments, while in Canada the geographic definition and size of only ten provinces give regionalism a cultural integrity and a political authority of its own.

Likewise, while both nations are federations, it is important to be mindful that federalism in Canada has evolved in a diametrically divergent direction from that of the United States. Whereas the American national experience began with a constitutional reservation to the states of all powers not specifically granted to the federal government, Canada (importantly influenced by the lesson, as she saw it, of the United States Civil War with its bitter issue over states rights) in 1867 wrote a precisely opposite premise into the constitution of her Confederation. Strange as it would surely seem to the founders of the two nations, the evolution of federalism in neither country has followed its original constitutional premise. The United States has gone far toward creating a dominant central government while Canada, at least as of the present, is seeking her national destiny by coming to terms with the increasingly powerful provinces through what is called "cooperative federalism" or "decentralized federalism." Whether these divergent developments are attributed primarily to the resiliency of geography or the perversities of history, they inevitably influence national approaches to an international relationship.

The relevance of this provincialism to contemporary Canada's search for viable *national* strategies was succinctly summarized by the late Howard Ross, recently dean of the faculty of management of McGill University: "No national strategies have any prospect of implementation in our country, unless the provincial governments are thoroughly committed to them—and this means they must participate in the drafting process. We have about come to the end of the line with programs worked out in Ottawa, and then 'sold' to the provinces." [3]

A prefatory word should also be said about the several hundred years of historical structure on which today's U.S.-Canada relationship rests. It is unfortunately quite unrealistic to assume that Americans approach the Canadian relationship with any real awareness that in this area of their foreign affairs history is a volcano alive with all the possibilities for explosive eruptions. It can, of course, be no part of this work's purpose to provide a shortcut to the full-bodied history of the relationship as it has been described in such a classic as J. B. Brebner's *North Atlantic Triangle,* but accepting the necessity for some perspective against which to consider the American presence in contemporary Canadian life, it may be that a few selected instances of the historical American presence will suggest how deeply rooted is the paradox of attraction, rejection, and ambivalence Canada's southern neighbor has always evoked.

No one has dealt more perceptively with this paradox than did Brebner, a native Canadian, later a naturalized American, who, as a member of the Columbia University history faculty, was for a long time the preeminent interpreter of Canada in the United States. His last work, published posthumously in 1960, went to the heart of the paradox with the opening observation that "perhaps the most striking thing about Canada is that it is not part of the United States." Having in mind the expansionist history of the American nation, Brebner went on:

It might be thought that the United States never wanted Canada, but the record reveals two American attempts to conquer it by war, two quite threatening and prolonged encouragements of filibustering against Canada, and an intermittent barrage of annexationist invitations, threats, and other devices lasting almost two hundred years.[4]

The two wars, of course, were the American Revolution and the War of 1812, both staples in schoolboy learning, but rarely featured in United States education as milestones in shaping the U.S.-Canada relationship.

In his lively social history, *Canadians in the Making*, A. R. M. Lower reminds us that the American Revolution played a critical role in creating Canada as well as the United States: "Two of the great formative experiences of English Canadians have been the English Conquest of French Canada and the American Revolution." [5] The American Revolution became significant to Canada because following the conquest of 1760, Quebec, while remaining almost wholly French in population, became another British North American colony and as such was soon a prime target for enlistment in the cause of the rebellious American colonies. In any event, the entire effort to export the Revolution proved to be a singularly inauspicious introduction of the American presence to Canada, a bad start that prepared the way for a legacy of distrust. The invitation to French-Catholic Canada, with revolutionary zeal and corresponding insensitivity, proclaimed the "rights of Englishmen" and abjured such "low-minded infirmities" as a "difference in religion" that might "prejudice you against a hearty amity with us." All the while, of course, England's 1774 Quebec Act was vigorously denounced by the Americans for its subservience to popery and its alleged extension of the boundaries of Quebec at the expense of the colonies to the south. As might be expected, the authority of the Quebec church and the land-holding seigneurs came down behind the authority of the British Crown; the *habitants*, on the other hand, in "the countryside" of eighteenth-century French Canada, were a more uncertain element. Basically submissive to the authority of their church and little drawn to "the rights of Englishmen," they were also mightily committed to a livelihood that, on occasion, while the going was good, could include hard coin from the realm of the Revolution which by mid-1775 had turned progressively from protest and politics to war.

Early in the war, Canada was the target of a loosely coordinated two-pronged invasion with Montgomery leading an American army down the Champlain-Richelieu route, an already ancient warpath, to capture Montreal and then down the St. Lawrence to join up with Benedict Arnold's legendary overland expedition to attack Quebec City, the citadel of Canada. The assault, made New Year's Eve 1775, was disastrously unsuccessful. Montgomery was killed, Arnold was wounded, and the repulsed American forces were left with an unpromising siege. Despite Benjamin Franklin's pilgrimage to Montreal (accompanied by an American Jesuit, a French printer, and others), to bolster the military effort, the American presence did not prosper. With the coming of the British navy in the spring to raise the siege of Quebec, a dispirited, disease-ridden American army withdrew from Canada, paradoxically leaving the country with a long British future because in 1776 the heart of Canada was French and Catholic, not English. The "neutral Yankees" of Nova Scotia also eschewed the Revolution.

Perhaps even more paradoxically, Canada's long British future became a lineal descendant of the American Revolution. Upwards of forty thousand loyalist refugees from the revolution became a founding force and a continuing anti-American factor in English Canada. American history has had no conspiracy of silence concerning the "loyalists," but until recently neither has it given much attention to the penalties and frequent outrages called down on them and their families by their opposition to the revolution. A more serious shortcoming is the fact that few Americans have had occasion to ponder the endemic rejection and distrust of things American which these thousands of aggrieved refugees, even as a progressively smaller portion of the population, injected into the heritage of English Canada. The influence of the loyalists on Canadian attitudes certainly contributed an anti-American element to Canadian nationalism. A. R. M. Lower spoke to this aftermath of the American Revolution when he wrote: "As an English population slowly gathered north of the line, it

inherited, not the benefits, but the bitterness of the Revolution." [6] And the durable quality of this heritage is testified to
in an observation of Lower's quoted by Brebner: "Canadians
are the children of divorced parents and they know the bitterness of a broken home." [7]

Undeterred by the negative reception of the revolution in
Canada, the unrequited courtship of the French Canadians,
failure of its military incursions, and the settlement of thousands of embittered American loyalist refugees in Canada, the
United States closed out its first generation of national life
with another and, as it proved, final military effort to conquer
Canada in the War of 1812. If anything, this second American
effort at military invasion ended in more ignominious frustration than the first, and even though the war itself was a
standoff, the result was historic for Canada: frustrating a
bumptious United States provided Canada, even as a British possession of loosely connected provinces, with its first
clear sense of self-conscious nationhood. In today's American
perspective the War of 1812 and its outcome were unimportant, but in the development of the U.S.-Canada relationship
the repulse by Canada of its more powerful neighbor's aggression (albeit again with more British power and leadership than
popular Canadian legend allows) was all but indispensable to
the eventual creation of an independent Canada. The Canadian perspective is well summarized by Professor Lower:

> The War of 1812, turning the people of the republic into
> foes, completed the separation which the War of the
> Revolution had begun, and confirmed Canadians in that
> determination on which their separate nationhood more
> than anything else has been built, the determination not
> to be "Americans." Without it, the long decades of
> peace might have served to heal the breach which the
> Revolution had created and to have made even Loyalists
> look with favour on the new state their old countrymen
> were building. With it, Canadians were quick to detect
> hostility in his glance. An event which goes far to explain
> the existence of two English-speaking peoples side by
> side cannot, therefore, be lightly passed over. [8]

In 1971, at the time of widespread protests in Canada against impending United States nuclear tests on Amchitka, many Americans were more than mildly mystified by a news report of a protest by a university group in western Canada that took the form of celebrating the War of 1812. Most Americans remember this unsatisfactory war principally for underdog naval victories, the burning of Washington by the British, and the fact that Andrew Jackson "won it" at New Orleans after it was, in fact, over. Few remember, if indeed they ever knew, that the torch was put to York (Toronto) well before the British followed suit at Washington, and fewer ever learned that Canadians regard the war as having taught the Yanks a lesson about not expecting to conquer Canada in a parade march. Even a mock celebration of the War of 1812 by Canadian students in 1971 is a significant reminder for Americans that, on the Canadian side of the relationship, history is never very far below the surface of any contemporary grievance. It was the judgment of the relationship's preeminent historian that "the War of 1812, more than any other single circumstance, nourished anti-Americanism as a basic element in both regional British North Americanism and future Canadianism." [9]

During the hundred years between the close of the War of 1812 and World War I, the United States became a great world power, Canada became an essentially independent nation, and the relationship of the two passed through an adolescence that, like most adolescent experience, had enough near misses in it to lend, at least in retrospect, a slightly miraculous aura to today's outcome. The peaceful division of a continent was accomplished despite the inflammable nationalistic politics of "manifest destiny" and annexation, rowdy border incidents, disputes about fisheries and trade, nation-rending internal crises, and the progressive withdrawal of Britain as a champion of Canadian interests, particularly in the 1871 Treaty of Washington and the 1903 Alaska Boundary Award.

Some Canadian scholars have seen this triangular development as one in which Canada simply passed from being a British colony through a brief interlude of independent nationhood en route to becoming a neo-colonial satellite of the United States. This gloomy view of Canada's destiny is far from generally accepted, but there can be no doubt that Canadians have never strayed far from the view that Canada's aspiration to independent nationhood has required a never-ceasing vigilance, almost like that of Holland as regards the sea, toward her dynamic neighbor to the south.

There is a substantial body of opinion, however, that credits the rise of an independent Canada more to American indiffer-ence than to either Canadian good management or friendly American intentions. One Canadian scholar, Professor Cole Harris, attributed such earlier American indifference to fun-damental geographic factors. When one remembers the crit-ical reaction in the United States to Seward's purchase of the Alaskan "ice box," it may well be, as he says, that "manifest destiny" was in reality more hot talk than cold calculation:

> ... it may be that the most important by-product of Canada's northern climate and early isolation from the United States has been American indifference to us. For all the declarations about "manifest destiny" by poli-ticians who envisaged the stars and stripes flying over a continent north of the Rio Grande, the wave of Amer-ican expansion which moved westward with inexorable force did not turn northward. British North Americans often feared American invasion, but Americans were not very interested in their northern neighbors. . . . While American sallies northward are emphasized in Canadian history, they are virtually absent in American, not because the Americans are trying to hide anything, but because northern objectives occupied little American at-tention. Had there been more agricultural land in Can-ada, or had the resources of the Shield been better known, American interst would undoubtedly have been greater; but, as it was, for most Americans 19th century Canada was a remote wasteland. . . . Canadians who are exasperated when American friends remark that they had not realized thee was "anything up there in Can-

ada," should consider the degree to which this American conception of Canada permitted Canada to exist.[10]

The "manifest destiny" of mid-nineteenth-century Canada, namely, annexation to the United States, never became official United States policy, and, in retrospect, it seems likely that Americans generally took less seriously than their Canadian counterparts the covetous sentiments that pervaded the rhetoric of American politics for several generations. Yet the fact is that Canadian apprehension of the United States during this period did become an abiding reality. It must also be said that Canadian apprehensions were based not only on American talk; border filibustering (private military freebooting) against Canada from the 1830s through the 1860s, first by the so-called Hunters' Lodges and subsequently by the Irish Fenian Brotherhood, gave substance to Canadian fears. Coming as it did on top of the two earlier invasion experiences, along with the rooted presence of loyalist sentiments, and coming at a time when Canada was moving toward the "new nationality" of Confederation, this apprehension definitely gave a cast of anti-Americanism to historic Canadian nationalism. The testimony of scholars and chroniclers is well-nigh unanimous that "Canadian national life can almost be said to take its rise in the negative will to resist absorption in the American Republic." [11] A perceptive Canadian journalist, the late Blair Fraser, put it thus in 1967: "Without at least a touch of anti-Americanism, Canada would have no reason to exist. Of all the general definitions of the Canadians, this is the most nearly valid: twenty million people who, for anything up to twenty million reasons, prefer not to be Americans." [12]

The validity of the judgment that historic Canadian nationalism is at heart a reaction to the American presence both south and north of the border can hardly be surprising to anyone familiar with the record. What is somewhat less generally recognized and acknowledged is that this negative attitude developed side by side with widespread borrowing and emulation throughout Canadian life of things American.

Canadian use of the American experience was not always uncritical and at times it, too, took the form of a negative judgment, but in the main it involved large positive inputs essential to the building of a productive society and independent nationhood on a continental scale.

Naturally enough, there has been less American influence in French Canada than in the English-speaking community, but even here there was apparently more of an osmotic transfer of basic political values than has often been assumed. Gustave Lanctot, a contemporary French-Canadian scholar, has concluded that American efforts to enlist Quebec in the American Revolution

> were instruments of political education for the people of Quebec. . . . They introduced to them the notions of personal liberty and political equality. American indoctrination taught Canadians their political alphabet and gave them their first lesson in constitutional law. . . . By opening the minds of Canadians to political ideas, it awakened in them a keener consciousness of the condition of the French element in their own country.[13]

These notions were again reflected and enlarged in the rebellions of 1837-39.

The rebellions of 1837-39 in both Lower and Upper Canada were indigenous, but the example of Jacksonian democracy was a stimulating, even a provocative, factor. In the end, comparison of the pros and cons of the two societies produced strong differences of opinion among Canadians and helped them to judge more perceptively the parliamentary, British-style "responsible government" they subsequently chose. Indeed, it was at this time, in 1839, that Lord Durham in his justly famed report on the rebellions (too little known to Americans) saw the pervasive impact of the American presence as the underlying reason for the development in Canada of a more dynamic, positive Canadian nationhood: "It is not politic . . . to allow the backwardness of the British Provinces everywhere to present a melancholy contrast to the progress and prosperity of the United States."[14]

The creation of today's Canadian nation was formalized by
the coming together in federal union (Confederation it was
called) of Nova Scotia, New Brunswick, and the newly divided
and designated provinces of Quebec and Ontario under the
British North American Act of 1867. Confederation itself was
in no small way an institutionalization of the Canadian concern and response to the American presence. In addition to
nearly a century of living with the ever-present centrifugal pull
to the south, and their cumulative apprehensions as to American intentions, Canadian leaders now had to reckon with a
heavily armed United States, victorious in a Civil War which
had dangerously embittered American-British relations once
again, with an inevitably unhappy impact on the American-
Canadian relationship. Likewise, there was the emotional ag-
gravation created by the Fenian raids and threats along the
entire eastern border. At the same time and somewhat related
to both the controversies of the war and the ill-founded notion
of some Americans that Canada's ripeness for annexation
would be hastened if she suffered economically, protectionist
sentiment in Congress had mustered the votes to terminate in
1866 the Reciprocity Treaty of 1854, an early landmark of
commercial cooperation between the two countries. And to
cap it all, the United States House of Representatives adopted
a resolution expressing its displeasure with Canadian Confederation, thereby providing Canadian leaders with convincing confirmation, if they needed any, of the wisdom of their
course.

From Confederation on, particularly after the triangular
settlement of the Treaty of Washington in 1871 and the
coincidental withdrawal of British armed forces from Canada,
the ultimate development of Canada as an independent nation became all but inevitable. Rejection of union with the
United States was already deeply embedded in Canadian attitudes, and the developing tendency of the British to settle
difficulties with the Americans at Canada's expense, if need
be, moved Canada toward independence from Britain in
several unplanned respects: first, peaceful relations between
the United States and Great Britain removed the historic
cause of United States armed conflict with Canada and Can-

ada's need for Britain's protection; second, triangular settlements at Canada's expense created a growing conviction that she could not afford to continue to rely on Britain to handle her interests vis-à-vis the United States. Both factors were present in the 1871 Treaty of Washington, particularly in the settlements as to the fisheries, the Alabama Claims, and its failure to deal with Canada's grievances from the Fenian raids. The decisive disillusionment of Canada with Britain as her champion, however, came in 1903. After some big-stick talk by President Theodore Roosevelt, Britain's Lord Chief Justice, Lord Alverstone, voted with the American members of a triangular tribunal settling the Alaska-British Columbia boundary dispute in favor of the United States, an affair that has been characterized as "next to the War of 1812, probably the most unfortunate single incident, the worst setback to reasonable understanding, in the whole gamut of Canadian-American relations." [15]

Elihu Root's initiatives as secretary of state brought United States-Canada relations back to a more positive posture. In particular, the 1909 Boundary Waters Treaty was a genuinely creative development, establishing the permanent International Joint Commission, an agency that proved highly useful in bringing a positive approach to boundary water problems, and which today is evolving into broader, usefulness as a collaborative facility for dealing with pollution. And yet within two years, in 1911, an internal Canadian political crisis which turned out the great French-Canadian Prime Minister, Wilfrid Laurier, brought a resurgence of traditional anti-Americanism. Under a banner of "no truck or trade with the Yankees," in a sort of delayed reprisal for United States denunciation of reciprocity in 1866, Canada rejected a major reciprocity arrangement that President Taft, at considerable political cost, had gotten approved by the American Congress. "In the most unexpected and dramatic reversal of their modern history, the people of Canada savored to the full the unprecedented joy of rebuffing their overpowering American neighbor." [16] Reciprocity was left an unwanted orphan by both countries for another quarter of a century.

The development of Canada as an autonomous, sovereign nation within the British Commonwealth is a major story in its own right, but it is assuredly a story that cannot be understood separately from the development of the Canada-United States relationship. Canada's independence came gradually as an evolving process rather than in the American pattern as a definitive revolutionary event. This gradualism has caused different chroniclers to perceive different dividing points in Canada's national development, but there is general agreement that by the close of World War I Canada's national development and the changing nature of the British Empire had combined to make Canadian nationhood an accepted fact in the international community. This new constitutional status was proclaimed at the 1926 Imperial Conference, and in 1931 the British Parliament's Statute of Westminster made the British Commonwealth of autonomous nations formal and final.

The American role in Canadian development up to World War I was summarized by Brebner in his binational view: "Any foreigner could tell them [Canadians] what they themselves felt compelled to deny—that the greatest force exerted on their development was the stimulating example of the people of the United States in adapting themselves to and mastering the North American environment. Canadians had proved eminently capable of doing this too, but the similarities between their performance and that of the Americans were so much greater than the differences that it was futile to try to separate them." [17] World War II changed little constitutionally, but it revealed a new reality that had been forming for a generation or more: the United States had replaced Britain as the dominant external influence in Canadian affairs. The two North American nations, with a minimum of critical scrutiny, now moved into a more comprehensive transnational relationship than any two independent nations had ever previously known.

Ten years after World War II, Canada's eminent economic historian, Harold Innis, took a gloomy view of this development: "The change from British imperialism to American has been accompanied by friction and a vast realignment of the Canadian system. . . . Canada moved from colony to nation to colony." [18]

As part of its continuity, history often modifies the judgments of historians; today we are required to know that neither Brebner's futility of separateness nor Innis's demise of an independent Canada are categorical imperatives in the contemporary United States-Canada relationship.

Notes

1. "Innovation in a Cold Climate: The Dilemma of Canadian Manufacturing," *Science Council of Canada*, Report No. 15, 1971, p. 30.
2. Carl Berger, "The True North Strong and Free," in *Nationalism In Canada*, Peter Russell, Editor (Toronto: McGraw-Hill, 1966), pp. 4, 24.
3. "Recent Development in Canada," Remarks to British-North American Committee, June 18, 1972.
4. J. Bartlett Brebner, *Canada* (Ann Arbor: The University of Michigan Press, 1960), p. ix.
5. A. R. M. Lower, *Canadians in the Making* (Toronto: Longmans, Green and Company, 1958), p. 135.
6. Lower, *Canadians in the Making*, p. 135.
7. Brebner, *Canada*, p. 105.
8. Lower, *Canadians in the Making*, p. 174.
9. Brebner, *Canada*, p. 116.
10. Cole Harris, "The Myth of the Land in Canadian Nationalism," in *Nationalism in Canada*, pp. 37-38.
11. S. D. Clark, "The Importance of Anti-Americanism in Canadian National Feeling," in *Canada and Her Great Neighbor*, H. F. Angus, Editor (Toronto: The Reyerson Press, 1938), p. 234.
12. Blair Fraser, *The Search for Identity: Canada, 1945-1967* (Garden City: Doubleday and Company, 1967), p. 301.
13. Gustave Lanctot, *Canada and the American Revolution* (Cambridge: Harvard University Press, 1967), pp. 225-26.
14. *Lord Durham's Report*, G. M. Craig, Editor, Carleton Library Series (Toronto: McClelland & Stewart, 1963), p. 129.

15. J. B. Brebner, *The North Atlantic Triangle*, Carleton Library Edition (Toronto: McClelland & Stewart, 1966), p. 264.
16. J. B. Brebner, *Canada*, p. 380.
17. Brebner, *Canada*, pp. 364-65.
18. Harold A. Innis, "Great Britain, the United States and Canada," in *Essays in Canadian Economic History* (Toronto: The University of Toronto Press, 1956), pp. 404-5.

CHAPTER 2

The American Economic Presence

"Canada, from the British Conquest on, had always been under the influence of the southern god. In every year of her history she has been 'Americanized.' " [1] Nowhere is the historian's judgment more vividly witnessed than in the contemporary tenor of an observation made in 1839 by Lord Durham, not a word of which would need to be changed if he were reporting today to Elizabeth II rather than a young Victoria:

> ... the influence of the United States surrounds him [the Canadian] on every side, and is forever present. It extends itself as population augments and intercourse increases; it penetrates every portion of the continent into which the restless spirit of American speculation impels the settler or the trader; it is felt in all the transactions of commerce, from the important operations of the monetary system down to the minor details of ordinary traffic; it stamps, on all the habits and opinions of the surrounding countries, the common characteristics of the thoughts, feelings and customs of the American people. Such is necessarily the influence which a great nation

exercises on the small communities which surround it. Its thoughts and manners subjugate them, even when nominally independent of its own authority.[2]

The American influence in an essentially isolated and rural Canada of 1839, omnipresent as it was in Lord Durham's observation, must have been a mere token of what has become reality in the late twentieth-century relationship of two technologically advanced, communication-intensive societies sharing cheek-to-jowl the North American continent. Indeed, the recent acceleration of change in this most fundamental feature of the relationship has been such over the past generation alone, that, for purposes of critical analysis and understanding, today's American presence must be approached as an essentially different phenomenon from even its pre-World War II dimensions.

Most contemporary extensions of the American economic presence can fairly be said to be in response to indigenous Canadian needs and wants. Today's American presence, however, also takes its character and significance from several developments which were essentially external to the bilateral relationship, namely, the Cold War and the drastic decline of Britain as a world power at the same time as the United States became a superpower. The Cold War brought about an unprecedented United States-Canada peacetime alliance with its integrated air defense of the continent; the transposition of Britain and the United States in world affairs saw the American presence replace Britain's historic hegemony on the Canadian scene.

It is not merely that trade and investment have multiplied many times with the quantum leap in commercial and financial activity that followed World War II in both Canada and the United States; it also is a reflection of technological advance in manufacturing, in transportation, and in mass-media communication. With these technological advances came a concomitant increase of cultural mobility involving persons, goods, information, ideas, and attitudes. While a panoply of economic, defense, cultural, and communication developments add up to a totality that Canada's militant nationalists lament as the "Americanization" of their country, this syndrome is best understood through awareness of its main components.

A. Trade and Investment

Among all the sectors that make up today's American presence, trade and investment are paramount by almost every consideration in the eyes of both Canadians and Americans. For purposes of perspective, it is essential that the specifics of analysis not obscure the fundamental structural features of the dominant position of the United States in Canada's foreign trade and foreign investment: in the early 1970s Canada imported from the United States upward of 70 percent of her total imports, and about the same percent of her exports went to the United States. The recent stability of this United States dominance on both the import and export side of Canada's foreign trade is indicated by the fact that for the six years, 1965 through 1970, her imports from the United States averaged about 72 percent of the total, while exports to the United States over the same six years averaged over 65 percent. Despite Canada's current aim toward more diversification in her trade relations and the American business recession, the United States percent of her exports in 1973 and 1974 remained in the 68 to 70 range while imports from the United States held close to 70 percent in both years. In Canadian dollars, Canada's 1973 imports from the United States were 16,484 million dollars, and her exports to the United States were 17,070 million dollars. For the first six months of 1974, the value of Canadian exports to the United States reached 10,165 million dollars, and imports 10,230 million dollars, projecting an annual total upward of 40 billion dollars [3]—by far the largest bilateral trade in the world.

It is instructive also to keep the United States side of the trading relationship in mind: in 1970, exports to Canada were 27.8 percent of the United States total, and our imports from Canada were only 21 percent of the total. In trade as in most things, the United States is critically more important to Canada than Canada can ever be to the United States. The trick is to be mindful of this comparative perspective while still being aware that Canada is by far both America's largest foreign market and its principal source of imported supplies.

American domination of foreign investment in Canada is even more pronounced than in foreign trade. The critical frame of reference is the overall consideration that 80 percent of the foreign control in Canada's basic industrial economy is exercised by United States-controlled firms,[4] a figure, incidentally, that while awesome enough, is very different from the seriously mistaken and widely repeated assertion in a well-known business review, that "U.S. industry now controls more than 80% of Canadian manufacturing." American control is, in fact, in the 50 percent plus range.

A meaningful perspective on the contemporary American presence in trade and investment should also include a more subjective background consideration that is too little taken into account: the fact that the rise of the United States to today's dominant position involved the displacement of the mother country not by just "some other" country or countries, but by the United States, a sort of "prodigal son" whose growing dominance in the affairs of an independent Canada inescapably evoked past apprehensions and sowed fresh concerns. The relatively sudden shift from British to American dominance in Canada's foreign trade and investment involved drastic changes in international trading patterns as well as internal Canadian adjustments.

During the early part of the twentieth century Canadian foreign trade (and indeed the United States-Canada relationship) found its basic balance in a triangular pattern whereby Canada's export surplus to the Great Britain offset a chronic deficit created by her surplus of imports from the United States. Following World War II, a pattern of greater bilateral balancing with the United States developed. Whereas in 1937 about 36-plus percent of Canada's exports went to the United States and 40-plus percent to Britain, by 1955 nearly 60 percent of her exports came to the United States and her British market had been more than halved, down to 18 percent. Canadian imports followed the same trend: 60-plus percent coming from the United States in 1937, and 73-plus percent in 1955, contrasted with a sharp falling off in her imports from

Great Britain for the same years, from 18-plus percent to only 8.5 percent.

The fact that Canada's trade with other Commonwealth countries followed broadly the same decline as that with Great Britain indicated that Canada's new trading pattern was more responsive to economic considerations than to political affiliations, including Commonwealth preferential tariff policies. In 1932, immediately after the formal establishment of the British Commonwealth of Nations by the 1931 Statute of Westminster, the Commonwealth countries negotiated an elaborate system of British Empire trade preferences aimed both at countering America's 1930 Hawley-Smoot tariff increases and at giving substantive cohesion to the Commonwealth concept. It is one of the intriguing paradoxes of that period and an instance of the perversity of which policy is capable that the preferential protectionism of the Ottawa Agreements contributed to the displacement of Britain by the United States as the dominant external factor in Canada's economic life. On the trade side, the Ottawa Agreements were a motivating factor in getting the American Reciprocal Trade Program launched in 1934, leading to the 1935 reestablishment of reciprocity in U.S.-Canada trade. In the foreign-investment sector, as a leading Canadian economist has said, British preferential protectionism brought "a new influx into Canada of United States branch plants to take advantage of the protected Canadian and Commonwealth markets." [5]

The development of foreign investment in Canada paralleled the drastic shift from British to United States dominance in trade: a reversal as between the United States and Great Britain investment positions of more than 100 percent in forty years. After World War II the change was precipitous. In 1941, 72 percent of total foreign investment in Canada was British, and 23 percent American; by 1954 the American share was 77 percent, while the British investment presence had fallen to 17 percent of the total [6] on its steady decline to today's 10 percent or less, against the United States 80 percent.

Economic nationalism, of course, made the establishment of branch plants in foreign countries attractive to all international businesses. American business, however, was uniquely ready with the capital, the technology, the management, and the entrepreneurial drive to take advantage of the especially attractive opportunity in Canada. A close-at-hand branch, with abundant raw materials and a minimum of foreignness, opened two doors: one into the protected Canadian market, the other into the preferential Commonwealth market. The outcome was sententiously summed up by Canada's eminent economic historian, Professor Innis: "Paradoxically, the stoutest defenders of the Canadian tariff against the United States were the representatives of American investors. Canadian nationalism was systematically encouraged and exploited by American capital." [7] The outcome might also be cited as a classical instance of economic nationalism hoist on its own petard. The multinational corporation, the foremost American presence in Canada today, is not, of course, a creature born of the Ottawa Agreements, but it surely was nurtured on them.

In breaking down the quantitative dimensions of today's American economic presence in Canadian life, it may be well to start near the top, namely the automotive industry. It is here that the American trade and investment presence approaches the zenith of transnational integration. The Canadian automobile industry is about 95 percent owned by American companies. Under the "free trade" in new automobiles and parts provided principally for the automobile manufacturers of the two countries by the Automotive Agreement of 1965, automotive exports have led all Canadian manufactured exports to the United States at a level that helped mightily to transform Canada's chronic trade deficit with the United States to better than a billion-dollar surplus in 1970; indeed, the turnaround in automotive trade alone between 1965 and 1970 went from an $800-million Canadian deficit in 1965 to a Canadian export surplus of over $300 million in 1970. In 1974 the picture changed again so that despite a continuing Canadian export surplus of completed vehicles, a deficit of $1.3 billion for Canada's total trade under the Auto Pact was caused by lower exports of parts.

Unique as it is as the major sector in the United States-

Canada trade relationship, and dominant as it is as an American manufacturing presence in Canada, the automotive industry represents only one vivid piece in the overall mosaic of foreign direct investment in Canada. The 1972 comprehensive study, *Foreign Direct Investment in Canada*, done for the Government of Canada under the supervision of Herb Gray, then Minister of National Revenue in the Trudeau government, showed the percentage of nonresident ownership actually

> is greatest in the petroleum and coal products industry (99.5 of assets). The others in which there is very great non-resident ownership include: rubber products (93.1), transport equipment (86.6), tobacco (84.3), and chemicals (81.5). In each case four fifths or more of the assets, sales, profits and taxable income are accounted for by non-resident ownership. Other industries in which non-resident ownership exceeded one half of industry assets include machinery, electrical products, and primary metals. . . . It is also evident . . . that the high technology industries are generally non-resident dominated.[8]

Nonresident ownership in mining is almost 63 percent of assets, greater than the nearly 60 percent for all manufacturing.

Keeping in mind the magnitude of foreign ownership and the finding of the Gray Report that "approximately eighty percent of foreign control over Canadian manufacturing and natural resource industries rests in the United States," [9] it is not surprising that American control of Canadian industries, estimated by book value of capital employed, is 45 percent for manufacturing, 60 percent for petroleum/natural gas, and 56 percent for mining/smelting.[10] Amidst the confused tangle of "dogs-compared-to-cats" data that has plagued the statistical picture of foreign investment in Canada, the foregoing is probably the most meaningful percentage profile available of the contemporary American direct investment presence. Mitchell Sharp, then Secretary of State for External Affairs, in presenting his authoritative view of Canada-United States relations in October 1972, rounded the statistics off with the conclusion that "American investment in Canada results in 50 percent American control of our manufacturing industries, with much higher percentages in particular sectors." [11]

Foreign long-term investments in Canada involve both portfolio and direct investment. In 1970, the combined total was estimated by the Bank of Nova Scotia at nearly 44 billion dollars. (All figures, unless otherwise noted, are Canadian dollars.) The 1970 estimate of 44 billion dollars, up from 6 billion dollars in 1926, included over 25 billion dollars of book value in foreign-direct investment and about 16 billion dollars of portfolio investment, with about 3 billion dollars in other forms of foreign holdings. Of the 25 billion dollars in direct investment, the American share was estimated by the B.N.S. at around 20 billion dollars;[12] it may have been somewhat larger. In 1972, Herb Gray's study group, while acknowledging the variations and difficulties involved in such calculations, concluded that "a figure a little below 30 billion dollars [in 1968] is a reasonable estimate of the book value of foreign controlled firms." [13] The American share, estimated at 80 percent of that figure, would have been about 24 billion dollars and seven years later, in 1975, allowing for internally generated Canadian assets as well as new external investment, this book value is probably upwards of $30 billion. At the end of 1972, United States Department of Commerce figures put it at nearly 26 billion dollars, as against 94 billion dollars throughout the world. Abraham Rotstein, a leading nationalist of the University of Toronto, estimated in 1972 that the market value of United States long-term investment in Canada was over 40 billion dollars.[14]

The salient fact is that the branch-plant sector of Canadian corporate activity has now acquired a vitality of its to the point where injections of foreign capital are no longer the sole or even the main source of growth in many of these enterprises. A Canadian subsidiary's ability to generate its own capital needs somewhat paradoxically gives the enterprise a Canadian viability of its own, while still expanding the foreign investment presence. Such indigenous expansion is particularly noticeable in the high-growth technological and extractive industries.

The Gray Report stated the outlook for nurturing the foreign-investment presence from Canadian sources with matter-of-fact bluntness:

> ... even if new foreign direct investment were to be entirely excluded from Canada, foreign control would continue to grow in absolute terms, due both to internal generation of funds by foreign controlled companies and by their ability to raise external funds in the Canadian capital markets ... over 60 percent of the financing for the expansion of foreign controlled firms in the 1961-67 period came from sources in Canada.[15]

In 1972, according to United States Department of Commerce figures, out of an increase in United States direct investment in Canada totaling 1.7 billion dollars, all but 380 million dollars, nearly 78 percent, came from internally generated reinvested earnings.

Although the Gray Report foresaw the continued growth of foreign direct investment, the critical overall proportion of foreign control in Canadian corporate activity has been relatively stable in recent years. In 1969, foreign-controlled corporations accounted for 35 percent of the total assets of nonfinancial corporations reporting under the Corporations and Labor Union Returns Act, about the same proportion as in 1968. This 35 percent represented foreign-controlled assets of 45 billion dollars, up from all sources by 3.6 billion dollars over 1968, with about three quarters of the increase in the manufacturing and mining sectors. In sales, foreign-controlled firms account for just about the same proportion, 36 percent of the total of 125.4 billion dollars. In net book profits and in taxable income the share of foreign-controlled firms was respectively 47 and 48 percent of the total, both also little changed from 1968.

The number of foreign-controlled corporations in nonfinancial industries was up about 10 percent in 1969 to a total of 5,556 firms, or 4 percent of all corporations; more significantly perhaps, 71 percent of the foreign-controlled corporations were 95 percent or more foreign-owned. In 1969, foreign take-overs of Canadian enterprises were particularly evident in asbestos, food and beverage manufacturing, forestry products, electronics, and steel.[16]

The continuing upward trend in new foreign investment was confirmed by a March 1972 report of *Statistics Canada:* foreign direct investment rose by roughly 25 percent in 1971 over 1970, increasing by 905 million dollars for 1971, as against 770 million dollars in 1970. The 1971 direct-investment net inflow was reported as the largest on record, with 65 percent of the total coming from the United States.

On the other hand, recent United States figures indicate that at least a temporary peak in new United States direct investment from net capital outflow going to Canada may have been reached: the 1972 net United States direct-investment input totaled only 380 million dollars, down from the 1969-70 level of over 900 million dollars; in the first quarter of 1973, the first-quarter figure was 77 million dollars, less than half for the same quarter of 1972. The potential strategic significance of these figures is suggested by the fact that they are against the trend of United States direct-invstment out-flows generally which for the first quarter of 1973 were 2,100 million dollars, up 1,400 million dollars over the first-quarter figures of the previous year.

The bulk of the new investment in recent years, 80 percent in 1971, went into petroleum, natural gas, and mining,[17] investment areas that until the last several years have been prime attractions for American capital for a quarter of a century. A shrewd Canadian observer, the late Blair Fraser, felt that "Labrador iron no less than Alberta oil changed the identity of Canada ... [and] also changed the balance of control in the Canadian economy. Not only in themselves but in the notice they attracted and the example they set, oil and iron brought American ownership and control into Canada on a scale never equalled before." [18]

Any profile of the American investment presence must take account of the fact that foreign investment, like most things in Canada, must be perceived in regional as well as national terms. Canadian nationhood is all but dominated—histori-cally, geographically, politically, and certainly economically—

by a resilient regionalism that at times seems to be Canada's salvation and at other times the nation's irremediable curse. However that balance be struck, it is a certain thing that regionalism cannot escape the shaping influence of the American presence. J. M. S. Careless, of the University of Toronto, lists among the impairments to building a modern Canadian nation "the evident fact that the United States ministers to sectional division in Canada. Pulls to the south ally the various Canadian regions with their more powerful American neighbors, thus thwarting the development of strong east-west ties within Canada herself." [19]

As might be expected, the American presence, as well as the Canadian response to it, varies greatly from region to region. Ontario, the region closest to the principal United States markets and their industrial activity, and itself the keystone of the Canadian economy, has a substantially higher proportion of foreign-owned manufacturing than any of the other regions. Over the four-year period, 1965-68, 70 percent of Ontario's corporate taxable income from manufacturing came from nonresident-owned companies. Over the same period, Ontario's share of Canada's total taxable income from foreign-owned manufacturing was nearly 60 percent, compared with less than 25 percent in Quebec, under 10 percent in the Prairie Provinces and British Columbia, and less than 3 percent in the Atlantic Provinces. [20]

Statistically and visibly, Ontario is incomparably the heartland of the American economic presence in Canada; indeed, 45 percent of "U.S. controlled manufacturing employment" in all of Canada is found within one hundred miles of Toronto. [21] Not surprisingly therefore, the same area is also the heartland of another well-established form of the American economic presence, the international labor union.

B. The Labor Union Presence

The American presence in the affairs of organized labor in Canada is large and long-standing; like trade and investment, it has chronically, and occasionally sharply, aroused nationalistic concerns for at least three quarters of a century. And like the American business presence, it is today under mounting attack from the militant nationalists. Affiliation with the large international unions based in the United States with their dominant American membership has been historically important in the development of organized labor in Canada. This affiliation has been challenged from time to time and in recent years its character has been modified in the direction of greater Canadian autonomy. But the fact remains, as the Canada Department of Labor has stated, that "a significant feature of the Canadian union movement is the predominance of so-called international unionism, namely unions with headquarters in the United States. . . . In no other country of comparable size and industrial importance does this phenomenon exist." [22]

Organized labor in Canada, upward of 2,500,000 members in 1973, represents nearly 29 percent of the total labor force. In 1971, 62 percent of Canadian union membership was affiliated with the United States-based labor organizations, but, as might be expected, the Canadian membership represented only about 6.5 percent of the total membership of the international unions. In only one moderately large international union, the International Woodworkers of America, has the Canadian membership predominated (51-plus percent in 1967); in 65 percent of the international unions the Canadian membership was less than 10 percent. The largest union in Canada for some years has been the United Steelworkers of America, which among the big internationals has also had the top Canadian membership of 12-plus percent. Other internationals in Canada's top five have been the Auto Workers and the Carpenters Brotherhoods; the Teamsters and the Brotherhood of Electrical Workers being in sixth and seventh place, with the Machinists ninth. [23]

During its long, prominent presence in Canada's labor affairs, American labor leadership from Gompers on, in collaboration with like-minded Canadians, has repulsed several challenges to the United States connection. These challenges have usually involved a mixture of nationalism and personal power struggles, often seasoned in earlier years with more than a touch of indigenous opposition to a strong labor movement, whatever its national character. Yet, certain fundamental factors kept the Canadian labor movement basically hospitable to the American affiliation. In the background is the fact that organized labor has had a traditional affinity for the concept and rubric of international affiliation. This orientation, along with the large role of American subsidiaries as employers of Canadian labor, made affiliation with the power and experience of United States-based international unions a natural and indeed a well-nigh necessary condition of life for Canadian unionism during the earlier period of Canadian industrial development. Until recently, most observers on both sides of the border have believed that this remained the essential reality and that there was little likelihood the American affiliation would be severed, at least so long as the American economic presence in trade and industry remained dominant. Today's new nationalism may be changing this prospect.

There are indications that today's American labor presence in Canada is losing strength in both size and influence. Membership in Canada's noninternational unions has been growing proportionately more than Canadian membership in the American international unions. In 1971, the membership of the internationals was down to 62 percent (lowest since 1939) from nearly 71 percent as recently as 1965. By 1973, membership in international unions with headquarters in the United States had fallen to 56.5 percent,[24] down 5.5 percent in two years.

Of greater immediate significance is the fact that the largest federation of unions in Canada, the Canadian Labour Congress (C.L.C.), comprising about 72 percent of the total membership of Canadian union members and with a majority of its membership affiliated with American unions (dominantly A.F.L.-C.I.O.), has been increasingly militant in urging, indeed requiring, greater organizational fiscal and policy autonomy on its member unions in their relations with the American internationals.

The Toronto *Financial Post*, in a 1972 report on "A Move Toward All-Canadian Unions," concluded that "The larger internationals in Canada now manage to stand on their own feet, although the U.S. subsidy was a prominent feature of

Canadian labour until the mid-1960s." [25] Many of the smaller internationals continue to lean heavily on their American headquarters for support and leadership. The trend in the larger unions, however, has been in the direction of Canadian autonomy.

Although the American affiliation has been under pressure from the new nationalism for some years, most labor leaders on both sides of the border have continued until very recently to support it strongly as a shared asset. The rise of the multinational corporation is increasingly cited as a compelling reason for strengthening labor's transnational collaboration. The American headquarters of the UAW is careful about respecting the autonomy of its Canadian members, but nowhere has the transnational collaboration of unions gone further than in the automobile industry where the principle of continental, as distinguished from national, collective bargaining seems now to be established. The special circumstances of this highly integrated industry make it unlikely that continental labor settlements will be followed widely in other industries, but isolated instances will probably increase.

Long before the multinationals became a prime concern, Canadian unions made common cause with their American headquarters in seeking comparable labor standards in wages, hours, and pensions, and in some cases outright parity with the United States. An officer of the Canadian Steelworkers union recently put this Canadian interest in the international affiliation in frankly nationalistic terms: "much extra profit—particularly profits of U.S. owned businesses—would have left Canada instead of staying at home in the form of bigger Canadian pay cheques had it not been for the extra bargaining power provided Canadians by their more than 13 million fellow-members below the line." On the American side, the big international unions, along with their overarching sense of labor solidarity, presumably have had a self-interest in a more prosperous Canadian customer for United States exports, a less dangerous lower-wage competitor in United States and world markets, and in not having Canada become a haven for "runaway" American enterprises.

In earlier years, sectors of the Canadian government as well as the Canadian business community, often including executives of American subsidiaries, manifested concern with an alleged role of the internationals in fomenting Canadian labor demands for parity with American levels, arguing that in many Canadian situations such levels were economically unwarranted and would work to the detriment of the Canadian national interest. This particular criticism of the American labor presence, which is little heard today, was more grounded in self-interest economics than today's broader nationalistic grounds of exorcising the American influence as a threat to an independent Canada.

Current opposition to the internationals increasingly centers on the American presence per se. As a result, the international unions, and particularly the Canadian Labour Congress, have had to face mounting criticism of the American connection from such centers of militant nationalism as the earlier "Waffle" wing of the New Democratic Party (N.D.P.), and the Committee for an Independent Canada. Perhaps more seriously, much the same generalized antagonism to the American presence is being voiced by nationalistic labor figures such as Ed Finn, research director of the Canadian Brotherhood of Railway, Transport and General Workers, who in 1972 disparaged C.L.C. leaders as "labor continentalists," asserting that "the debate over Canadian union autonomy is . . . a reflection in miniature of the broader debate now raging over Canada's uncertain future as an independent nation." [26] The influential, nationalistically oriented *Toronto Star* welcomed "signs that organized labor in Canada is beginning to realize its responsibility to the defence of an independent Canada." [27]

In 1971, provoked by the August 15 action of President Nixon in imposing a surcharge on imports, the Canadian Union of Public Employees, the second largest union in Canada and a noninternational C.L.C. member, demanded by formal resolution a loosening of economic ties with the United States, and sharply criticized Ottawa for permitting American domination of the economy. Later the Canadian Labour Congress itself became a powerful voice calling for federal action to screen new foreign investment as well as take-overs of Canadian enterprises, a major policy extension the Trudeau government adopted after its electoral setback in 1972. The C.L.C.'s economic policy committee asserted "total disenchantment" with the government's 1972 proposal for screening foreign take-overs: "It is no exaggeration to say that this government policy does not begin to deal seriously with the question of foreign ownership and control of the Canadian economy." [28] The C.L.C.'s strongly stated concern for national economic independence and its avowed fear that Canadians will become more and more subservient in their own house testified to a weather change in the nationalistic sentiments of Canadian unionism since only a few years ago, when a critical observer wrote that "the Canadian Labour Congress is dominated completely by its American affiliates." [29]

In 1974, the Canadian Labour Congress became sharply more militant about autonomy for its affiliates. The Vancouver annual convention, led by a nationalistically oriented "reform" movement, spearheaded by the powerful noninternational, the Canadian Union of Public Employees, prescribed a program of autonomy for the C.L.C. international affiliates which, if enforced as authorized, could drastically alter the American affiliation pattern of Canadian unionism.

During 1974 a major disengagement did occur when the Canadian members of the United Paperworkers International Union voted to terminate their affiliation, a decision accepted at the international's headquarters as ordained by today's Canadian nationalism but not as precluding a looser cooperation in the future.

The full impact of the C.L.C.'s new autonomy rules is yet to be seen, but there will be difficulties, e.g., the international president of the Association of Plumbers and Pipefitters indicated that Canadian members would have to choose between the union's constitution and the C.L.C.'s new rules. [30]

The movement toward greater autonomy of the Canadian unions, however, faces little resistance from the industrial-union leaders in either Canada or the United States. Such resistance will likely center in the craft unions, especially in construction. There is clear evidence, however, that some of the big Canadian affiliates, for example, the United Auto

Workers, are not prepared to take nationalistic actions considered detrimental to the union's own interests. In early 1972 the "Waffle," then the left wing of the N.D.P., initiated a proposal to have the auto workers engage in a work stoppage to protest any possible weakening of the so-called Canadian safeguards in the Auto Pact with the United States. The proposal was ignored by the union, but its Canadian Director, Dennis McDermott, seized the opportunity to castigate the Waffle leaders as "footloose academics with no affinity with and little understanding of labour" who were trying "to penetrate labour." More importantly, Mr. McDermott used the occasion to make it publicly and painfully clear that the N.D.P. should be rid of the Waffle element, an exodus that later ensued. The union adopted its own approach for the protection of Canadian auto workers, and the international secretary-treasurer assured the Canadian Council of the U.A.W. that the international considered the Auto Pact "good for the union workers on both sides of the border." [31] It is noteworthy that the international headquarters of the U.A.W. has scrupulously respected the autonomy guidelines laid down by the C.L.C.

Prominent United States labor leaders have sought to counter the indictment of the nationalists that the American labor affiliation is inimical to the Canadian national interest and the self-interest of Canadian labor. On May 12 and 13, 1972, *The Toronto Star* and *The Globe and Mail,* two of Canada's principal newspapers, carried these headlines: "Halt Multi-National Firms: Unionist," and "U.S. Quotas to Exempt Canada, Abel Says." The *Star*'s lead paragraph reported I. W. Abel, president of the United Steelworkers of America, as telling the Canadian policy conference of the union that multinational corporations must be stopped from buying up another country's industry and using resources without regard for the interests of its citizens. He saw the role of international unions as weapons to counter the threat of the multinationals: "They have helped us both build and protect the standard of living for working people that is respectable in both our countries"—all safe enough gospel but sufficiently targeted on current Canadian concerns to earn a subhead from the *Star:* "A blow for Canada."

The American labor leader, however, had a much more powerful "blow for Canada" which he produced in a *Globe and Mail* interview the next day: "Mr. Abel said many of the international unions affiliated with the AFL-CIO would make representations on behalf of an exemption for Canada from any quota system should the [Burke-Hartke] bill now before Congress be enacted." It would be hard to make the American affiliation look more attractive to a Canadian union whose two hundred delegates had earlier deprecated the protectionist policies of the international union as being an ultimate threat to "the continental solidarity of the international union in general" but who also, without the benefit of Mr. Abel's "blows for Canada," had rejected, with only three dissenting votes, a proposal "to establish a completely Canadian independent steel union."

Intervention by international unions in the United States on behalf of Canadian interests is not unprecedented: previous trade-policy interventions have involved the steelworkers and the International Woodworkers of America. The negotiation of the Auto Pact in 1965, with its prospects of important benefits to Canada, was supported by the U.A.W. as a good thing for both countries in the face of congressional concerns that Canada might get the lion's share of the benefits, a position the international has continued to maintain despite United States official dissatisfaction in 1971 with the pact's operation. Inescapably, the internationalism of the big unions will be put to the test on trade policy in the years ahead, and nowhere more sharply than under the critical scrutiny of their Canadian affiliates. The protectionist position of the A.F.L.-C.I.O. under George Meany's leadership has raised widespread concern on the Canadian labor scene. The position of American labor on trade policy may or may not be decisive in determining the future of the American affiliation of Canadian unions, but it will be a big factor. More importantly, it is likely that the high visibility of the American labor presence and its involvement in Canadian nationalism will make the position of American labor on United States trade policy a factor in the affairs of the relationship that will reach out far beyond the affiliation question itself.

In 1959, Dr. Eugene Forsey, then Director of Research for the Canadian Labour Congress and more recently a highly respected member of the Canadian Senate, undertook what has proved to be a farsighted examination of "the influence of American labor organizations and policies on Canadian labor." Taking account of the forces of geography and history that bind the two societies, he saw no possibility that, with or without organizational ties, the influence of American labor on Canadian labor, "like the influence of American everything else on Canadian everything else," could be anything but enormous. At the same time, even as he made the case for the American affiliation in labor's self-interest, and even as he dismissed the danger of any threat to the practical independence of the Canadian unions (let alone to independent nationhood), he acknowledged that one of the principal guarantors of this autonomy "is the growth of Canadian nationalism in Canadian unions. . . . They are jealous of the autonomy and equality which now exists between the C.L.C. and the AFL-CIO, and of the Canadian sections of international unions. They will defend it against any encroachments." [32]

The outlook for international unionism in Canada was seen in much the same way in 1967 by John Crispo, Canada's foremost student of the subject. In his authoritative work, *International Unionism, a Study in Canadian-American Relations*, Professor Crispo saw the position of an international unionism threatened by only

> two interrelated possibilities. . . . Should an extreme form of nationalism come to the fore, the members of international unions would probably take a second look at their American affiliation [and second] the attitudes of international unions themselves. The future of international unions in Canada probably depends more than anything else on their willingness to adjust themselves to the Canadian fact. [33]

Eight years later the record reveals both a heightened Canadian nationalism and, on the side of the international unions, a developing "willingness to adjust themselves to the Canadian fact." The outlook for continued formal affiliation is at least uncertain, but many American and Canadian labor leaders still hold a shared sense of self-interest in maintaining some degree of international affiliation. The effectiveness of these adjustments in harmonizing the American affiliation with the "Canadian fact" may provide a useful reading on changes in other privately governed areas of the relationship where the "Canadian fact" will require accommodation.

It needs hardly more than mentioning that the American presence in Canadian associations is not confined to organized labor but is to be found in every area such as churches, universities, learned societies, professional and business organizations, sports, and service clubs. Indeed, an inventory of such organizational affiliations would be a formidable introduction in both breadth and depth to the American cultural presence in today's Canada.

Notes

1. A. R. M. Lower, *Canadians In The Making* (Toronto: Longmans, Green and Company, 1958), p. 441.
2. Lord Durham Report, G. M. Craig, Editor, Carleton Library Series (Toronto: McClelland & Stewart, 1963).
3. Source: Statistics Canada, Summary of Foreign Trade, June 1974, Table 4, and *Canada Weekly*, Aug. 28 and Sept. 4, 1974.
4. *Foreign Direct Investment in Canada* (Ottawa: Government of Canada, 1972), p. 16.
5. John J. Deutsch, "Recent American Influences In Canada," in *The American Economic Impact on Canada*, H. G. J. Aitken et al., Editors (Durham: Duke University Commonwealth Studies Center, 1959), p. 38.
6. The Bank of Nova Scotia *Monthly Bulletin*, March 1958, in Aitken et al., *The American Economic Impact*, Appendix, Table 9, p. 157.
7. Harold A. Innis, "Great Britain, The United States and Canada," in *Essays in Canadian Economic History* (Toronto: The University of Toronto Press, 1956).

8. *Foreign Direct Investment,* pp. 19-20, hereafter referred to as the Gray Report. Corporations and Labor Unions Returns Act (CALURA), 1968 Report.

9. Gray Report, p. 5.

10. Ibid., p. 20. It should be noted that this study reveals no substantial difference as between American "control" and ownership in manufacturing; however, in petroleum/natural gas American ownership at 51 percent is nine points lower than the control figure and five points lower for mining/smelting, also at 51 percent.

11. Toronto speech, October 18, 1972.

12. The Bank of Nova Scotia, *Monthly Review,* April-May, 1971.

13. Gray Report, p. 18.

14. *Independence the Canadian Challenge,* Abraham Rotstein and Gary Lax, Editors (Toronto, 1972), p. 79.

15. Gray Report, p. 26.

16. *Canadian Weekly Bulletin,* Vol. 27, No. 14 (Ottawa: Dept. of External Affairs, April 5, 1972). Source: CALURA.

17. *International Canada,* Toronto: C.I.I.A. (March 1972), p. 53.

18. Blair Fraser, *The Search For Identity: Canada, 1945-1967* (Garden City: Doubleday and Company, 1967), p. 72.

19. *The New Romans,* Al Purdy, Editor (Edmonton: M. G. Hurtig Ltd., 1968), p. 133.

20. Gray Report, pp. 22-24.

21. Philippe Garigue, *Science Policy In Canada* (Private Planning Association of Canada, 1972), p. 5.

22. *Union Growth in Canada* (Ottawa: Canada Department of Labor, 1970), p. 36.

23. *The Labour Gazette,* March 1972, p. 140, and *Union Growth,* p. 93.

24. *Canada Weekly,* Aug. 28 and Sept. 4, 1975, p. 8.

25. The *Financial Post,* Toronto, March 18, 1972, p. 20.

26. "All-Canadian Unions Are Vital In The Fight For Our Independence," article by Ed Finn, *The Toronto Star,* March 18, 1972.

27. *Toronto Star* editorial, December 11, 1971.

28. *Globe and Mail,* May 17, 1972.

29. I. M. Abella, "Lament for a Union Movement" in *Close the 49th Parallel, Etc. The Americanization of Canada,* Ian Lums-

den, Editor (Toronto: University of Toronto Press, 1970), p. 90.

30. *The Financial Post*, Toronto, June 8, 1974.
31. *The Toronto Star*, January 17, 1972.
32. *The American Economic Impact on Canada*, pp. 127-47.
33. John Crispo, *International Unionism, A study in Canadian-American Relations* (Ontario: McGraw-Hill Company of Canada, 1967), p. 322.

CHAPTER 3

The Cultural Presence

American economic and cultural presences are inseparably intertwined in Canadian life, but the perception that Canadians have of them as concerns of Canadian nationhood varies. Contrary to the counsel of Professor Kenneth Galbraith of Harvard as "an advisory Canadian," most nationalistically aroused Canadians seem more concerned about the economic than the cultural Americanization issues; at the same time they tend to regard American direct investment as far more dangerous than even a 70-percent American trade exposure, largely because it is perceived as a bearer and begetter of American cultural contamination.

Trade, particularly in a country as heavily dependent on exports as Canada, is popularly perceived as a domestic boon, the producer of jobs and national income (imports being a necessary evil). Foreign direct investment, on the other hand, in the form of the multinational enterprise, introduces into the nation's daily life a phenomenon whose description, a "foreign-controlled company," is vulnerable to instinctive xenophobia. The presence of such enterprises in large numbers brings foreign bosses, foreign attitudes, foreign ways—in short, a complex of influences and interests which, taken together, can readily appear in the eyes of a beholden beholder to be foreign exploitation, i.e., "neo-imperialism."

Concern about this spin-off impact of the American direct investment inescapably fuels the apprehensions of Canadians. The Gray Report focused its investigation on the various ways in which this impact might adversely influence Canadian life; except for the potential extraterritorial application of American antitrust and trading-with-the-enemy laws, the record is sparse as to objectionable actions directly attributable to the American business presence. The Report found, however, that "a foreign controlled company acts as continuous transmission belt and that the cultural impact is greater than simply the impact of the initial investment." Indeed, it was the judgment of the Report that because of the special circumstances of the United States-Canada relationship this spin-off presence has a singularly serious impact on Canada:

> The penetration of Canada by foreign direct investment, particularly from the United States, has been facilitated both by the lack of a strong sense of Canadian national identity and by the cultural similarities between Canada and the United States. Control of a substantial portion of Canadian business activity by United States corporations is likely, in turn, to have a significant impact on the Canadian cultural environment. There is a "continuous feedback" relationship between foreign direct investment and Canadian culture, with cultural similarities facilitating foreign direct investment and foreign direct investment, in turn, inducing greater cultural similarities. . . . It can be asserted with some degree of confidence that the presence of large volumes of foreign investment concentrated in United States hands increases the difficulty of developing a distinctive Canadian culture.[1]

Many a bored journalist has turned out a piece depicting how hard it is for the American visitor to believe he is in another country until he sees the movielike version of a Royal Canadian Mounted Police officer on view in front of the parliament buildings. The language, the talk, the architecture, the advertisements, the automobiles, the stores, the food, the newsstands, the books, the magazines, the TV, the sports, the dress, the credit cards, even the gripes, have a pleasant or painful, as the case may be, high content of familiar home feeling about them. Perhaps the most significant clues to cultural assimilation are the "in" jokes, a true witness of cultural sharing. During the Nixon presidency an official Report of a Committee of the Canadian Senate, for example, in the course of sharply condemning the pervasiveness of American cultural penetration, found the following parody irresistible: "Let us now, in the words of one authoritative source, make One Thing Perfectly Clear." [2] It would be hard to cite stronger proof of the extent to which the American cultural presence pervades Canadian life. Conversely, the one-way cultural sharing in the relationship is revealed by one's realization that the most uproarious take-off on Trudeau would of certainty play to a deadpan audience in the United States.

There is, of course, no clear-cut division between the American cultural spin-off that comes as a byproduct of economic activity, and those cultural transmitters such as books, magazines, and the mass media, of which more will be said later, that to some extent would be on the Canadian scene regardless of other forms of the American presence. There can be no separation of the indirect from the direct in the importation of cultural influences—as in biology, like begets like and an American presence in one area will attract an American presence in other areas.

A. Visitors and Immigrants

Even today, when technology has revolutionized the process of acculturation by permitting human experience in the form of ideas and knowledge to move and be shared independently of the movement of persons, the transnational flow of Canadians and Americans remains a major factor in transmitting American culture into Canadian life. Unless energy shortages intervene, upward of seventy million travellers annually will move back and forth across the border. In 1972 30.5 million returning Canadians and 36.2 million visitors entered Canada from the United States. Whether the traveler be an American or a returning Canadian, the asymmetries of the relationship are such that the flow of cultural influence is almost exclusively northward. The average input into Canadian life from incoming Americans and returning Canadians approaches two hundred thousand persons daily. Actually, the single most significant witness to the grass-roots, person-to-person integration of the two societies may be the fact that about two thirds of the Americans and 75 percent of the Canadians cross to the other country and return the same day.

The immigration pattern between the two countries appears to be changing. In 1970-71 it moved from a chronic Canadian emigration surplus to a balance of about twenty-five thousand persons going to each country; since 1972, Canadian emigration to the United States has been significantly lower, falling to only some seven thousand in that year while immigration from the United States continued upward reaching 26,541 in 1974. Of itself, this movement of permanent residents probably has less cultural influence than the massive transient flow. Many recent emigrés to Canada, particularly those who wanted to escape American military service (probably fewer than twenty-five thousand), have gone for reasons of dissatisfaction with the United States, a circumstance that presumably reduces the likelihood of their being bearers of an infectious American presence. On the other hand, a nationalistically aroused writer recently characterized contemporary American immigration into Canada from "the social blight in the United States ... [as] the crowning threat because it undermines the foundations of the Canadian culture." [3] This is not, however, a widely expressed view and it probably takes less than adequate account of the natural desire of most immigrants, especially those who come with the zeal of converts, to become a part of their newly chosen national home on its own terms.

The foreigner abroad is, of course, a worldwide scapegoat and the United States-Canada relationship cannot expect to be free of this phenomenon. It is one aspect of the relationship that is best taken for granted. TV advertising and the full-page spreads run by Ontario and other provinces in American publications, luring Americans to a land that is "friendly, foreign and familiar," often seem a little incongruous when appearing cheek-by-jowl with complaints that Americans are taking over Canadian recreational areas. Most Canadian provinces are legislating against foreign purchasers of land, a policy characterized by a Vermont editor as "depressingly similar to the German philosophy of 'lebensraum.' " [4] At the same time in the United States north country the Canadian visitor's dollar is wooed with fluttering maple-leaf flags, even as "wild Canadian drivers" are the talk of the town in a Vermont community where summer-home purchasers have been predominantly Canadian.

B. American Academics

American teachers in Canadian universities are a form of the American presence that recently became a prime target of Canadian nationalism. A decade or two earlier, a common Canadian complaint was the so-called brain drain whereby Canada was said to be losing her promising intellectuals to American university faculties and other professional or artistic opportunities. In recent years the brain drain has been superseded by a reverse flow of intellectuals, regarded by some as a tidal wave of American Ph.D.s engulfing the faculties, particularly the social-science departments, of Canadian universities. This threat has been portrayed by two concerned Canadian academics under the rather Orwellian rubric: "The Universities: Takeover of the Mind." [5]

This particular American take-over apparently shares five characteristics in common with certain other take-over problems: (1) sweeping charges are difficult to evaluate; (2) the take-over in part involves the substitution of the United States for Britain as the principal foreign source of supply; (3) there is a substantial element of self-interest protectionism involved; (4) there is a decided difference of opinion among Canadians about the national interest; and (5) good, bad, or simply necessary, it came about largely in response to Canadian initiatives and needs. This issue is unlikely to suffer from anything resembling benign neglect since it directly involves the heartland of today's nationalism, the Canadian academic community.

Messrs. James Steele and Robin Matthews of Carleton University, whose Jeremiah-sized fears foretold a take-over of the mind, estimated that the proportion of Canadian faculty in Canadian universities diminished by about 25 percent between 1961 and 1968, largely due to United States imports; as a cure, they urged "legislation of a hortatory nature . . . to ensure that Canadians remain or eventually become a clear two-thirds majority of full-time faculty members in each department." While their statistics and conclusions have been contested, as aroused nationalists they take no comfort from the argument of others that an overall proportion of possibly 15 to 20 percent Americans is not a serious threat: "Without for a moment underestimating the serious threat of concentration by any non-Canadian group in Canadian educational life, the unique quality of U.S. participation must be seen clearly for what it is, in relation to . . . the general deluge of Americanization in Canada." [6]

The latter observation makes explicit an aspect of Canadian concern that is insufficiently appreciated by most Americans who, having little occasion to consider the full spread of the American presence, tend to approach each aspect on its individual merits. Concerned Canadians, on the other hand, are increasingly inclined to see individual aspects of the American presence not as isolated phenomena but rather as something that must be judged cumulatively as a part of the totality of the Americanization syndrome.

Recent studies done in both Canada and the United States indicate that the concern about American academics centers on the teaching of political science and sociology, subjects in which a possible threat to Canadian viewpoints and values (if not jobs) is greater than in the physical sciences. Canadian investigations, as well as a recent inquiry undertaken by Messrs. Kornberg and Tharp of Duke University, suggest that perhaps 35 percent of the personnel in sociology, and about 26 percent in political science are United States nationals. Nationalistically inclined academics tend to deprecate the "universalism" and behavioristic orientation of these imported

American scholars and, probably with more justification, their frequent lack of familiarity with the Canadian fact. The Kornberg inquiry revealed little doctrinal orientation attributable to nationality per se. Rather, the professional orientation of Canadian as well as American academics tended to reflect their graduate training, which for both groups had been mostly in American universities. The supply problem frequently led senior Canadian academics to turn to their own American graduate schools in recruiting junior personnel.

The explanation for the increase of American academics in Canada, especially during the sixties, as Canadian academic administrators have long recognized, was Canada's imperative need for more faculty, particularly in the social sciences, than were then being produced in Canada. There simply was no other source of supply than the American academic marketplace which was ready and able to meet this demand.

Kornberg and Tharp concluded that

> the concern voiced over the Americanization of Canadian universities has its origins in the enormous growth that higher education in Canada experienced in the post World War II period ... the number of doctorates produced in political science, and particularly in Canadian sociology departments, could not begin to keep pace with the tremendous expansion in faculty that was required because of increased student enrollments.[7]

The figures leave little doubt that the demand for faculty far outran the supply available in Canada during the 1960s. A Canadian account, based on data cited by President E. H. Petch of the University of Waterloo, reported: "Enrollment in Canada of full-time university students increased from 158,388 in 1963-64 to 270,093 in 1968-69, a total increase of ... almost 70% in a 5-year period. But between 1963 and 1968, Canadian universities awarded Ph.D.s to only 3,741 candidates in all fields, leaving about 7,500 additional academic vacancies to be filled from other sources." [8]

A 1973 statement by the Council of Ontario Universities documents its judgment that during the 1960s "the number of qualified Canadians available for university posts was grossly inadequate" to meet the great expansion in university enroll-ment. While reporting a large growth in graduate degrees, the statement also notes that shortages continue in the humani-ties, social science, and health-science fields. According to the same source, "By 1970 the citizenship of faculty in Ontario universities was: 61% Canadian, 15% U.S., 12% U.K."—12% others. The selection policy of the Ontario universities ac-cording to their Council should be to identify "Canadian experience and knowledge" as qualifications where these are relevant "for the particular post." Basically the same policy position was taken in Alberta in 1972 by a special committee appointed to investigate the controversy in that province.

Despite the now somewhat exaggerated threat of the American academic presence, at least on its statistical and educational merits, it would be a mistake to dismiss the con-troversy as an inconsequential campus tempest. Even if, as seems likely, this American influx proves to have been more inevitable than inimical, the hue and cry it has called forth casts a special light on the "anti-Americanism" component in today's nationalism, and thereby illuminates the vulnerability of an expanding American presence in its totality, regardless of the merits of particular aspects.

Professor Kornberg, the principal author of the Duke study and himself no stranger to the Canadian scene, posited a more disquieting explanation for "the quantitative and qualitative changes in anti-American feelings that seemingly have oc-curred during the last decade," and which have focused on United States nationals in Canadian universities as "highly visible and convenient objects against whom Canadian col-leagues can vent their hostility." Underlying a normal "his-torically rooted 'anti-Americanism'" and a measure of familiar job "protectionism," he found a more fundamental cause: "It is against the conditions symbolized by the term 'Amerika' that many Canadian academicians really are pro-testing when they charge that Canadian universities are being Americanized ... the underlying objection is to the United States as a society!" [9]

There can, of course, be no definitive validation of this

subjective explanation for the special hostility that the American academic presence seems to have called forth. Such hostility could also, at least in part, be the rationalized reaction of a particularly articulate group to the total Americanization syndrome. But whatever the degree of rationalization, the deeper disillusionment is undeniably present. The societal concerns of academics everywhere are likely to be somewhat ahead of the general community, as well as more sharply articulated, and it may well be that the hostility of a substantial portion of the Canadian academic community is a distant early warning that should be taken more seriously in both societies. Certainly, the temper of many Canadian campuses today makes clear that nationalistic concerns of "Americanization" cannot be dismissed solely at the level of quantitative analysis, or even by weighing the qualitative pros and cons of a particular American presence. Every form of the American presence abroad will increasingly be regarded as answerable for American society. To a degree, however, certain American academics have been especially vulnerable to Canada's "new nationalism." The university community's acerbic view of "Americanization" has undoubtedly been heightened by those American academic imports whose knowledge of Canada was less than minimal, itself a reflection of the fact that the Canadian presence has until very recently been all but nonexistent in American academic programs.

C. The Media

If it is in the nature of things national and human that immigrant American teachers should be regarded as intellectual retailers whose competition is unfair and whose professional orientation is too American, or too universal, to be compatible with a Canadian view of Canada, one would expect to find more widespread concern with United States publications and mass media as wholesale importers of the American cultural presence. In fact, this concern permeates Canada and, indeed, has been promulgated in official statements and policies for over two decades.

Print, as one of the most common and powerful means of

cultural transmission, is never far from the center of any discussion about the health of a national culture. Contemporary Canadian nationalism has concerns on various fronts, but none is at once more embattled and perplexing than the American dominance of the reading fare, other than newspapers, of Canadians. American affairs are ubiquitous in the news and editorial columns (not to mention the comics) of Canadian newspapers, and there is a limited but important circulation by mail and metropolitan newsstand sales of such American newspapers as *The New York Times* and *The Wall Street Journal*. But the Canadian income-tax disallowance of advertising expenses incurred in foreign-controlled publications has precluded the establishment, since 1965, of foreign control of Canadian newspapers and magazine enterprises. Likewise, the nature of newspapers and the restrictions on their advertising prevent large-scale importation, such as is possible in the case of American books and overflow magazines.

Books

Newspapers aside, the United States in one form or another is incomparably the principal supplier of Canada's reading materials.

Two thirds of the value of all books bought in Canada in 1969 was accounted for by imports, 80 percent of which came from the United States; nearly half of all United States book exports go to Canada. On the sensitive issue of foreign control of publishing enterprises, an Ernst and Ernst study done for the Canadian government in 1969 showed over 80 percent of the dollar value of Canada's English-language publishing done by foreign-controlled firms; broken down, "the Canadian-United States-United Kingdom ratio was calculated to be 19-59-22." [10] This foreign ownership ratio has since been somewhat changed. In 1970, two Canadian-owned firms, W. J. Gage Textbook Division and the Ryerson Press, were sold to the American firms of Scott-Foresman Company and McGraw-Hill, respectively, and in 1972, the Macmillan Company of Canada, a British-owned subsidiary, was acquired by the Canadian firm of Maclean-Hunter, bringing under Canadian ownership one of the largest book publishing operations in the country.

Magazines

The presence of American periodicals in Canada, which involves about four out of five magazines read by Canadians, takes two forms: first, the so-called American-magazine overflow, an essentially unrestricted volume of imported American editions which, however, since 1965 are required by the Customs Act to be free of advertising directed at the Canadian market. About 90 percent of Canada's total imports of periodicals comes from the United States and represents nearly 70 percent of United States-periodical exports to all countries. Second, and more acutely at issue, has been the dominating presence by special dispensation of the Canadian editions of *Time* and *Reader's Digest*, the latter having a widely read edition in French as well as English. Although for reasons of business self-interest, as explained below, most major Canadian periodical publishers were until recently inclined to live with the special status of *Time* and *Reader's Digest*, their dominance, along with the American periodical imports, has been increasingly viewed by many nationalists as a threat to the integrity of Canadian culture, and even to independent nationhood.

In 1970 a Special Committee of the Canadian Senate, under the chairmanship of the Honorable Keith Davey, produced a strongly stated affirmation of the critical importance to Canadian nationhood of Canadian-owned periodicals: "Magazines are special. Magazines are the only national press we possess in Canada.... In terms of cultural survival, magazines could potentially be as important as railroads, airlines, national broadcasting networks, and national hockey leagues. But Canadian magazines are in trouble." [11]

Lacking anything approaching a national newspaper, it was not surprising the Davey Committee found that nearly four out of ten Canadians over age fifteen received a news magazine, and that these tended to be the better-educated people with an annual income then of at least 12,000 dollars. Over half of these Canadians read *Time*. *Newsweek*, unlike *Time* and *Reader's Digest*, not having an edition published in Canada, got about one seventh of *Time*'s readership with its imported American edition.[12]

The Davey Committee Report (a paragon of readability among official reports anywhere), attributed the "palsied state" of the Canadian periodical industry primarily to the overflow circulation from the United States:

> Unhampered by tariff barriers, by language barriers, or by any form of protective legislation, foreign magazines —mostly American, naturally—pour into the country by the tens of millions (130.5 million copies in 1969), swamping our newsstands and occasionally overloading our postal system. . . . *Playboy*, to cite one example, collects about as much money selling its magazine in Canada as do the seventeen largest English-language consumer magazines combined. . . . We buy more than sixteen times as many copies of *National Geographic Magazine* as we do *Canadian Geographic*. We spend more money buying American comic books than we do on seventeen leading Canadian-owned magazines.[13]

Leaving aside what the *Playboy* figures may witness as to "continentalism" or even universalism of taste, they do testify that, as is true in nearly all other forms of the American presence, American periodicals are massively present in Canada because there is a widespread demand for them. Parenthetically, one cannot help pondering the possibility that such figures may tell fully as much about the potential outer limits of nationalism in the relationship of these two countries as does the interdependence of their economies.

As with other forms of the American presence, the provincial breakdown of the American magazine presence adds a special significance to the above national picture. In Ontario, for example, the total dollar value of magazine subscriptions and single copy sales in 1971 was reported by the provinces

Royal   Commission   on   Book   Publishing   to   be $45,932,235—only $3,609,277 (7.88 percent) of which represented sales of Canadian-owned magazines.

However massive the cultural and commercial impact of imported American periodicals, since 1965 they have been barred by law from competition for the Canadian advertising dollar. In Canada as in the United States, television is the magazine's most deadly competitor for a place in the advertising sun. In fact, it was the ability of *Time* and *Reader's Digest* to meet this TV competition that kept their Canadian editions, at least relatively speaking, *persona grata* with major periodical publishers in Canada. Their success gave magazines generally a credibility as an advertising medium that they might not otherwise have had in competition with television. As their success attests, these magazines would be formidable competitors on   their   merits   anywhere;   in   Canada   their strength has been backed editorially and financially by the parent American companies, while their special status under Section 19 of the Canadian Income Tax Law protected them against   the   possibility   of   other   Canadian   editions   being created by American competitors.

Time and *Reader's Digest* long dominated magazine advertising in Canada. The two magazines together in 1974 received nearly half (56 percent in 1969) of the 39 million dollars of advertising revenue accounted for by all major consumer magazines, *Time* earning $10.8 million and the *Digest*, 7.9 million dollars. And in national readership once again it is no contest—*Time-Canada* with a circulation in 1975 of about 550,000, has twice the readership of all its competitors combined. *Reader's Digest* blankets the nation in both English and French with a total circulation of about 1,500,000, which according to *Digest* estimates reaches six million readers monthly. In 1975, as will be explained hereafter, the outlook for these magazines changed abruptly and drastically.

Broadcasting
American-produced books and magazines provide weekly or monthly reading fare for thousands of Canadians. But the

American presence on Canadian TV and radio reaches a daily audience of millions. True, the Canadian Broadcast Act of 1968 expressly excludes the entry of American-controlled enterprises into Canada by prohibiting more than 20-percent foreign ownership of any broadcasting licensee, but, alas, for the long reach of this law, its grasp is limited by geography and the nature of the business. This inescapable Canadian fact of life was noted by the 1965 Fowler Committee on Broadcasting: "Any Canadian system of regulation can affect only part of the programming available to Canadians." American stations were even then within the reach of 54 percent of all Canadian television households and, as in other areas, this national average obscured significant regional variations, estimated even in 1965 to be 77 percent in Ontario, 68 percent in Manitoba, and 84 percent in British Columbia.

This extraterritorial American presence, estimated by some as now reaching 80 percent of Canada's TV audience, is powerfully augmented by the importation of American programs by Canadian stations. The government-owned C.B.C., as well as the private C.T.V. network and cable TV, import American programs for at least 40 percent of their broadcasting time. This is necessary to meet the pronounced preference of Canadian viewers for American programs, a preference which the Davey Committee reported in 1970 to be 71 to 24 percent in favor of American shows on the part of the English-speaking viewers.

No one has pictured the American presence in the form of transborder broadcasts more vividly than Chairman Juneau of the Canadian Radio-Television Commission (C.R.-T.C.):

> With all the talk about television programs eventually being available from one country to another by [satellites] . . . countries are having a lot of discussions as to what things would be like when direct broadcast satellites start operating. My answer is simple: it would be close to the present situation in Canada. As a matter of fact, it would take some time before things, in other countries, reached the point where they are in Toronto, Vancouver,

Hamilton, London, Windsor, or anywhere in Canada where there is cable television, like Montreal, Victoria, Winnipeg or Quebec City." [14]

The "present situation" in Toronto was summed up by a 1973 banner headline: "How Much Canadian TV Does Toronto Watch? Very Little." According to this *Toronto Star* study, a survey by the Canadian Bureau of Broadcast Measurement revealed that in evening prime time:

Three hours of every four in front of the screen here were spent looking at U.S. programs . . . while we have an array of Canadian stations here filling less than half their time with U.S. programs, we have just as many popular Buffalo stations showing All-American. And the Toronto situation is not a bad sample of the national scene . . . Canadian programming exclusive of news and sports (especially hockey), from 5 to 11 p.m. over an average week, draws only 13 percent of the viewing. . . . This drops to a tiny 9 percent in the more concentrated "prime" time of 8 to 10 p.m.

Mr. Juneau's Commission is quoted as agreeing with these findings. "But the federal broadcast czar was stubbornly optimistic when presented with *The Star's* figures. . . . 'Even at this level [he said], it's infinitely better than what's been accomplished in the movies.' " [15] A modest claim, indeed, and in itself a sufficient comment on the omnipresence of American movies in Canada.

Despite the Broadcasting Act, the determined efforts of the regulatory authorities, and the C.B.C.'s manifest sense of mission (some think too manifest) to "contribute to the development of national unity and provide a continuing expression of Canadian identity," the American broadcasting presence remains a major challenge for Canadian cultural nationalism just because it is not a major concern of the Canadian audience—the classic example, perhaps, of the "hang-up" Canadian nationalism so often encounters.

The Canadian Radio-Television Commission has used unsparing candor in reporting this problem. In its 1969-70 Report it said:

> The "Americanization of the [Canadian] unconscious" as well as risks for viability and future development of the Canadian Broadcasting System, appeared just two years after the latest Broadcasting Act a more imminent danger than it did in 1968.

The Commission further cited these facts: "Some 32 U.S. stations radiate across the Canadian border and 71% of the viewing public watch TV from both the U.S. and Canada." The 1970-71 Report again featured a deteriorating outlook—"Penetration of American stations into Canada by a combination of natural overflow of free-air American broadcasting and importation of signals by CATV [cable] have increased."

The full impact of cable television is still to be seen, but even by 1970 it was painfully clear to the C.R.-T.C. that "the problem is especially acute in Canada. Cable television has grown more rapidly here with the result that most of Canada's larger cities are within reach of U.S. television signals." [16] This technological extension of TV's reach is being countered by requiring priorities for Canadian programs and an effort to strengthen the quality and appeal of Canadian TV. Despite these and other steps by C.R.-T.C., the outlook is for an expanding American video presence throughout Canada.

If, as Chairman Juneau recently told a Toronto audience, Canada "is by far the most interesting mass-communication laboratory in the world," it is largely because in this respect Canada is also a country with little prospect of a narrowly nationalistic answer to the question he puts: "Can Canadians accept to be a minority voice in their own country?" [17]

Notes

1. *Foreign Direct Investment in Canada* (Ottawa: Government of Canada, 1972), pp. 297-98.
2. *The Uncertain Mirror,* Report of the Special Senate Committee on Mass Media, Vol. I (Ottawa: Government of Canada, 1970), p. 10.

3. D. W. Carr, *Recovering Canada's Nationhood* (Ottawa, 1971), p. 68.

4. *The Valley News*, White River Junction, Vermont, June 22, 1974.

5. Article by James Steele and Robin Matthews in *Close the 49th Parallel, Etc., supra*, p. 169.

6. *Close the 49th Parallel, Etc.*, pp. 171, 174.

7. Allen Kornberg and Alan Tharp, "The American Impact on Canadian Political Science and Sociology," in *The Influence of the United States on Canadian Development*, R. A. Preston, Editor (Durham: Duke University Commonwealth Studies Center, 1971), p. 89.

8. Ruth Lor Mulloy, "The 'Americanization' of Canada's Universities," in *International Educational and Cultural Exchange* (Winter 1971.), p. 9.

9. Kornberg and Tharp, "The American Impact," pp. 96-98.

10. *Publisher's Weekly*, April 5, 1971, pp. 29-30.

11. *Mass Media*, Vol. I, Report of the Special Senate Committee on Mass Media (Ottawa: Queen's Printer, 1970), p. 153.

12. *Mass Media*, Vol. III, p. 13.

13. *Mass Media*, Vol. I, p. 156.

14. Talk by Pierre Juneau, Chairman C.R.-T.C., Empire Club, Toronto, February 24, 1972.

15. TV feature story by Jack Miller, *The Toronto Star*, January 13, 1973.

16. Canadian Radio-Television Commission, '70-'71 *Annual Report*, p. 23.

17. Talk by Pierre Juneau.

CHAPTER 4

The American Military Presence: Canadian Bargain and Concern

Few Americans, even those with professional knowledge of Canada, think of the United States-Canada defense alliance as a potentially powerful element in the Americanization syndrome of contemporary Canada. Most Americans who think of it in Canadian terms regard the underlying alliance and its joint air defense, the North American Air Defense Command (NORAD), as a national-security bargain that Canada derives as an incidental benefit from her geographic location. It comes to Canada at relatively low cost, simply because the deterrence, the detection, and the defense the United States must provide for itself is, perforce, continental.

If a bargain it be, it is also "geographic justice" since any threat to Canada derives largely from her geography as the nuclear boundary between the two superpowers. The Minister for Defence, James Richardson, put Canada's security strategy thus:

> Canada's overriding defence objective is to prevent nuclear war ... The way we stop nuclear war today is by deterring the attacker ... and the way we achieve that is

by having any attacker know that North America can survive an attack and still have a retaliatory capability that can destroy the attacker.[1]

The Standing Committee of the House of Commons on External Affairs and National Defence, in an April 1973 report, while accepting the basic military rationale for NORAD, added:

> The Committee has concluded that one of the basic justifications for continued membership in NORAD is that it helps Canada avoid being faced with a request from the United States for facilities in Canada, the granting of which might impinge (or at least be considered by some Canadians to impinge) on Canadian sovereignty.... While there may be a need for some foreign military personnel to be stationed on Canadian territory, they should be kept as few in number as possible.[2]

The United States-Canada alliance for the joint defense of North America, a far more informal arrangement than NATO, has always maintained a comparatively low military profile. The Permanent Joint Board on Defense (P.J.B.D.), established by the Ogdensburg Agreement in August 1940, is little known outside official circles; the North American Air Defense Command (NORAD), created in 1958 with a common defense plan and a joint command under an American Commander-In-Chief and a Canadian Deputy-Commander, has operated from headquarters in the United States. It has received little public or political attention except for two brief but acute controversies in the early 1960s, related to the handling of the Cuban missile crisis and nuclear warheads for Canada's Bomarc missiles. Most importantly, perhaps, American military personnel stationed in Canada in connection with NORAD now total about two hundred, and their physical presence in connection with the various warning systems, the air-support facilities, and the high-altitude surveillance flights have generally been inconspicuous to the civilian population. Moreover, on the economic side, a cumulative Canadian surplus of sales, totaling about 500 million dollars, from defense equipment sold to the United States under the 1959 Defense Production Sharing Agreement, has muted nationalistic criticism, except for the NDP on the far left of the political spectrum, and a somewhat more general concern about Canada's role as a supplier of the United States at the time of the Vietnam war.

And yet, despite the easy acceptance of NORAD today as attested by a virtually uncontested renewal of the arrangement in 1972 for two more years and again in 1975 for five years (subject, however, to termination on one year's notice), Americans would do well to be sentitive to the possibility that, within the foreseeable future, the alliance could become the target of the mounting militancy in Canadian nationalism. Indeed, in this matter the primary potential Canadian concern is not the physical manifestations of an American presence, but the alliance itself, with its foreign policy implications and its inescapable aura of dependence. Other forms of the American presence are of more immediate concern, but since they are woven into the daily fabric of millions of private lives they may prove more difficult to eliminate or modify than the existing military collaboration. The possibility of such a development is grounded in the reality that today's alliance, a relatively recent and unprecedented form of peacetime collaboration in the relationship, was fashioned out of a perception by both countries of a common external danger, a perception now dimmed by détente, particularly in Canada. Once again, the perspectives of history are relevant.

During the first third of the twentieth century, the earlier view of Britain as defender of Canada was gradually supplanted by a developing assumption, as Prime Minister Laurier put it early in the century, that "the Monroe Doctrine protects us against enemy aggression." [3] With the rise of the Axis Powers, President Franklin Roosevelt gave explicit assurance, notably at Kingston, Ontario, in 1938, and then in the Ogdensburg Joint Defense Agreement of 1940, that the United States was prepared to protect Canada from external aggressions.

From World War II on through Korea, the Cold War, and the advent of intercontinental bombers and missiles, this Monroe Doctrine form of United States protection evolved into a jointly shared conviction that Canada's collaboration was important, perhaps essential, for the effective defense of the United States. Canadian leaders likewise had no doubt that the defense of their nation depended upon an effective American defense against what was then commonly perceived as the Soviet threat. As late as 1964, a Canadian White Paper speaks of "partnership with the United States in the defence of North America," explaining that "the emerging direct threat to North America itself . . . led to the concept of partnership with the United States in North American Air Defence, a relationship which was formalized by the signing of the North American Air Defence (NORAD) Agreement in 1958." Although the Trudeau Government's 1971 White Paper, *Defence in the '70s*, pointedly followed the lead of its 1970 foreign policy White Paper in eschewing the rhetorical embrace of "partnership" for the more guarded relationship of "cooperation," the view is still maintained that "in the defence of North America, Canada is inevitably closely associated with the United States." Incidentally but perhaps not inadvertently, Mr. Richardson, Canada's Minister of National Defence returned, albeit sparingly, to the terminology of "partnership" in his strong endorsement of an extended renewal of NORAD in 1975.

As Roger Swanson, an American student of the subject, has noted, "NORAD's history is . . . one of perpetual battle against shifting threat perceptions and technological obsolescence." [4] The Soviet threat from time to time is viewed differently in the two countries and the limited defense capabilities against missiles have tended to bring the effectiveness of the arrangement in question. At the same time, the mounting cost of upgrading detection and defense technologies has created serious funding problems for both countries.

NORAD's renewal in 1973 for only two years (the original term was for ten years, the first renewal for five) was acknowledged to be a holding action that in a clouded period kept options open. The 1975 renewal was supported by the Trudeau Government on much the same grounds as previous renewals but with a new emphasis on the desirability, as Minister Richardson put it, "to provide the continuity required for effective forward planning." A Canadian commitment to longer-range cooperation in continental defense would have a potential significance for the relationship well beyond defense. As the Minister testified before the House of Commons committee, a major factor favoring renewal was the larger consideration:

> Considerable importance is attached by our United States friends to the principle of continued Canadian cooperation ... through the renewal of the NORAD. Canadian willingness to renew the Agreement would therefore have a positive impact on Canadian-U.S. relations at a time when a number of difficult issues have to be settled between the two countries.[5]

It probably is not far from the truth to suggest that this consideration and the fact that the United States bears the principal portion of the defense costs Canada would otherwise face, continue to be dominant factors in Canada'a decision. Basic to the continuing alliance, however, is the reality that neither country can be free of underlying security concerns. Détente with the Soviet Union is still in an early testing stage, and while any movement away from cold-war policies encourages public optimism, hard-core security concerns of the cold-war period will continue embedded in a permafrost of distrust for years yet. Indeed, it is entirely possible that within several years, regardless of the course of the détente, the two countries may revise the concept of a joint air-defense command into a broader arrangement involving closer collaboration on anti-submarine warfare and related matters.

As Minister Richardson observed in his 1975 parliamentary testimony, the NORAD agreement clearly needed updating, "to reflect the significant changes, particularly in the strategic situations which have occurred" since 1958, with the replacement of the bomber by intercontinental missiles as the

primary nuclear threat. Although Canada has had no commitment to participate actively in a positive ballistic missile
defense and the principal missile detection sites (BMEWS)
are located in Alaska, Greenland and England, through her
NORAD arrangements Canada does participate in the comprehensive space monitoring operations carried on by the
United States at its space defense center at Cheyenne
Mountain. If the missile threat continues to mount, particularly as it involves submarine launched missiles and mul-
ti-targeted warheads, a meaningful Canadian contribution to
the future missile defenses in whatever form, whether through
NATO or NORAD or both, would require close, sophisticated defense collaboration with the United States.

Despite these considerations looking toward the continuation of a strong American presence in Canadian security programs, it is far from unthinkable that world affairs as well as
the relationship itself might develop otherwise so as to bring a
loosening, or even eventual termination, of the defense alliance. The involvement of the United States in military actions of which Canada strongly disapproved could precipitate
a re-examination of the alliance by Canada. It is also conceivable that today's spreading nationalism could itself
become so anti-American as to produce the same result. Even
though the 1973 and 1975 renewals of NORAD evoked virtually no political dissent, the defense alliance has been meeting enough skepticism, including limited but sharp attack
from Canadian intellectuals, to suggest that this form of the
American presence may not be beyond the reach of the still
incoming tide of the new nationalism. In these circles there is a
continuing and spreading sentiment that military alliance
with the United States is a handicap, and perhaps even a
barrier to full Canadian independence. In this view, the
defense alliance tends to "Americanize" Canada'a perception
of the international community and to handicap her pursuit
of greater independence and diversification in her foreign
relations.

Likewise, the more militant nationalists, particularly those
committed to an all-out socialist ideology, see "continentalism" in economics and "continentalism" in a military al-

liance as mutually reinforcing forms of American domination. The Defense Production Sharing Agreement of 1959 is regarded by such critics of the alliance as having become "even more than NORAD ... a symbol of Canada's growing involvement in America's imperialist policies through the mechanism of continental defence, and an acid test of the political subordination that follows in the wake of military and economic subordination to a great power." [6]

Such a fulminating indictment still speaks for only a small minority of Canadians, but it does suggest the potential explosiveness of even a relatively inconspicuous American military presence in the context of high nationalistic emotion. Any foreign military presence, however well handled and even when based on genuine agreement, must always reckon with its dangerous potential as a detonator of collected grievances in the host country. As the fear of external danger dissipates, the frustration of not being in charge of one's own defense can provide a potent psychological rallying point for other nationalistic grievances; at that point any foreign military presence literally becomes a "hostage to fortune." That the American military presence in the defense of Canada is not immune to such concerns was authoritatively, albeit mildly, suggested by Prime Minister Trudeau on no less noteworthy an occasion than his visit to Moscow in May, 1971:

> Canada has increasingly found it important to diversify its channels of communication because of the overpowering presence of the United States of America and that is reflected in a growing consciousness among Canadians of the danger to our national identity from a cultural, economic and *perhaps even military point of view*. It has been the desire of the Canadian people and certainly reflected by this government to, I repeat, diversify our points of contact with the significant powers in the world. (Italics supplied.)

Mr. Trudeau's instruction of the Russians on Canada-United States relations was not roundly applauded back home. His remarks were viewed by some as egregiously unnecessary while others dismissed them, especially the reference to the military aspect of the relationship, as the offhand utterance of a politician abroad. The subsequent record, however, suggests that these observations accurately reflected the responsible judgment of Canada's leadership.

In October 1972, the Secretary of State for External Affairs, Mitchell Sharp, in his carefully considered statement on "Options for the Future" regarding the United States relationship, observed that:

> In a Canada undergoing profound and rapid changes . . . there has been a growing and widely-felt concern about the extent of economic, *military* and cultural dependence on the United States, and the implications for Canadian independence. . . . Defence cooperation between the two countries remains firmly anchored and close, but the momentum of the Fifties and Sixties toward closely-integrated and structured defence arrangements has abated. (Italics supplied.)

The defense alliance, like other sectors of the relationship, will certainly undergo significant change during the next decade; it is in no immediate danger of dissolution but "the jury is still out" on its future as a fundamental feature of the Canadian-United States relationship. Although Canadian opinion, both generally and in official pronouncement, remains committed to close cooperation with the United States as Canada's most effective contribution to mutual nuclear deterrence, a different view is occasionally heard. As the Honorable Douglas Harkness, a prominent Progressive Conservative, put it, "Canada must begin to develop . . . a set of functions which, through the use of Canadian airspace, geography and warning facilities, will help to communicate to *both* superpowers that no attacks are contemplated when they are not being contemplated." [7] Movement in this direction would hardly be welcome in United States defense circles, but it would not be a startling policy projection of the neutralist sentiment conspicuously present in Canada's new nationalism.

Here, as elsewhere in the relationship, however, developments in the larger international community will powerfully, perhaps decisively, influence North American security arrangements. If NATO holds and prospers, Canada is unlikely to risk creating fresh misigivings concerning the importance she attaches to this European connection. And whatever form it takes, the collaboration of Canada and the United States in the defense of North America will be essential to an effective NATO.

At the same time, if the foregoing observations of Messrs. Trudeau and Sharp forecast as well as record Canadian national sentiment, and most especially if East-West tensions continue to ease, Americans should probably be prepared for further abatement, as Mr. Sharp gently put it, of "the momentum . . . toward closely integrated and structured defence arrangements." Any significant modification of the defense alliance one way or the other will likely signal and influence the direction of the relationship in other policy areas.

No certain new direction is signaled by the 1975 renewal of NORAD, but a more cautious Canadian stance, at least in political sentiment, seems evidenced both by the rejection of Minister Richardson's preference for an "indefinite renewal" and by the conspicuous emphasis in the report of the House of Commons Committee on the need for further close scrutiny of NORAD's future.[8]

*   *   *   *   *   *   *

Whether geographic, historic, economic, cultural, or in defense of the continent, as a Canadian scholar has observed, "To a large degree the American presence has shaped Canada. . . . One is tempted to conclude, in fact, that there could be a Canada without the United States—and may not be a Canada with one." [9] The preceding chapters sketch the dimensions of the problem; Parts II and III present possible approaches for managing, not resolving, this continental-sized paradox.

Notes

1. House of Commons, Standing Committee on External Affairs and National Defence, No. 9, April 13, 1973, p. 6.
2. House of Commons, Standing Committee, No. 10, p. 7.
3. Quoted by J. B. Brebner, *North Atlantic Triangle*, Carleton Library Edition (Toronto: McClelland & Stewart, 1966), p. 277.
4. "NORAD Origins and Operations," *International Perspectives* (Ottawa: Department of External Affairs, Nov. 10, 1972), p. 3.
5. House of Commons, Committee on External Affairs and National Defence, Issue No. 3, February 27, 1975, pp. 12-13.
6. Philip Resnick, "Canadian Defence Policy and the American Empire," in *Close the 49th Parallel, Etc.*, p. 109.
7. "Defence in the 70s: Comments on the White Paper," *Behind the Headlines* (Ottawa: Canadian Institute of International Affairs, October 1973), p. 14.
8. House of Commons Standing Committee on External Affairs and National Defence, Second Report on North American Air Defence Agreement, Issue No. 14, April 22, 1975.
9. J.M.S. Careless, in *The New Romans*, Al Purdy, editor (Edmonton, Alberta: M. G. Hurtig, 1968), pp. 132-134.

PART II

The Canadianization of Canada

CHAPTER 5

Nationalism: Premises and a Shifting Spectrum

Nationalism as "devotion to or advocacy of national interests" becomes even relatively precise only in a particular context. Canadian nationalism is a very different thing from French-Canadian nationalism, and then, of course, there are the subdesignations such as economic nationalism and cultural nationalism. Many Canadians who today characterize themselves as nationalists speak of their concern as the "new nationalism," but even among this group there are significant variations of style and intensity. The occasional use here of "militant nationalist" will designate, albeit loosely, those whose nationalistic concerns are strongly, often even stridently, manifested.

A further complication arises from the need many, perhaps most, Canadians sincerely feel to insist that their particular nationalism is not to be confused with "anti-Americanism." And yet, as nearly all students of the relationship have recognized, Canadian nationalism as an articulation of Canada's nationhood has always had at heart, as Professor Lower put it, "the determination not to be 'Americans.'" In that elemental sense, Canadian nationalism can hardly avoid being in some degree anti-American. Such anti-Americanism need not be, and rarely is, malevolent or even unfriendly, but it is a first premise, perhaps even a categorical imperative of Canadian nationhood that merits more awareness on the part of Americans.

For purposes of this study, unless otherwise clear from the context, Canadian nationalism, whatever its subdesignation (except French-Canadian nationalism), refers to an articulated concern for national cohesion and independent nationhood, particularly independent of American hegemony, as a prime value of Canadian life. There is rarely any great difficulty in distinguishing this kind of endemic anti-Americanism, if such it be, from the virulent kind. The latter is, of course, also a reality, but it is not a majority sentiment in Canadian society generally. More vociferously there is also an angry, ideological anti-Americanism which is motivated by what its followers call "the struggle for an independent and socialist Canada." This point of view on the radical outer edge of today's nationalism contemptuously dismisses all Canadian political parties, including the N.D.P., for their acceptance of "liberal democracy". The enmity of this ideological nationalism focuses on capitalism and also on international unionism as "a keylink in the system of U.S. domination of Canada . . . [and for] its constant export of labour conservatism to Canada." [1]

As for the ideological component of Canada's nationalism, it is well for Americans to be aware that socialism is more readily accepted as a normal part of the political scene than is true in the United States. The N.D.P., with its "liberal-democracy" brand of socialism, is explicitly identified with organized labor and has considerable strength in the universities; even without its left-wing "Waffle" element the N.D.P. is the principal political stronghold of militant nationalism. In 1975, the N.D.P. controlled the provincial governments of Manitoba, Saskatchewan, and British Columbia, but the return of the Trudeau Liberals in July 1974 as the majority party effectively removed the N.D.P., at least for some years, from the influential position it had held in Parliament for two years as the balance between the deadlocked Liberals and Progressive Conservatives.

The flavor of the far left's militant nationalism is witnessed in the "Waffle Manifesto" of 1969, principally credited to Professor Melville H. Watkins of the University of Toronto, who, incidentally, only a year previously had chaired a Task Force commissioned by Lester Pearson's Government to report on Foreign Ownership and the Structure of Canadian Industry:

> The major threat to Canadian survival today is American control of the Canadian economy. The major issue of our times is not national unity, but national survival, and the fundamental threat is external, not international.

> The American empire is the central reality for Canadians. . . . the essential fact of Canadian history in the past century is the reduction of Canada to a colony of the United States.

> So long as the federal government refuses to protect the country from American economic and cultural domination, English Canada is bound to appear to French Canadians simply as part of the United States.

Such belligerent rhetoric is little, if at all, reflected in the increasingly nationalistic temper of public policy, but it leaves no doubt that the far left is committed to a nationalism that is conspicuously anti-American in form and basically ideological in impulse. While this brand of ideology has little appeal to most Canadians, its nationalism does reach out toward the more traditional concerns of many Canadians.

The nationalism of the Canadian business community, while hardly capable of being as craven before the American presence as the socialists assert, is, of course, much influenced by business interests. In some situations, especially in the past, this interest has undoubtedly muted nationalistic sentiments but more recently the opposite is true. Increasingly, contemporary considerations make it "good business" for Canadian enterprises to project a more self-conscious nationalism than is commonly the case in most other industrial societies. This tendency is increasingly conspicuous in the advertisements of both American subsidiaries and Canadian-owned enterprises. For example, the largest Canadian-owned publishing conglomerate ran an advertisement under the heading "Call Canada Collect," mentioning Canada or Canadians six times in a text featuring the message that it is "a totally Canadian company" where "when you call Maclean-Hunter Limited you can't get a better Canadian connection." The entire spread was decorated with seven small Canadian flags and the firm's name was punctuated with the mapleleaf symbol in place of the usual hyphen. A vivid but not extraordinary example of the "background nationalism" that is increasingly evident on the Canadian business scene in competitive confrontation with the American presence.

Even though the contemporary American presence is increasingly perceived as a syndrome of interacting influences which, taken as a totality, suggest to many Canadians the "Americanization" of their country, Canadian reaction is nevertheless still far from being monolithic. It ranges across the spectrum from an idealized "continentalism," through a "so-what" pragmatism coexisting with the rising national consciousness, to an outer-edge rejection of all things American as being by definition (and history) the antithesis of all that Canada is or should aspire to be. While neither end of this spectrum has ever attracted a large proportion of the Canadian people, there can be little doubt that for over a decade now there has been a significant, continuing shift of majority sentiment toward a more cautious, a more critical view of the Canada-United States relationship. For the foreseeable future, the dominant mood of contemporary Canada will continue to shift toward a more self-conscious nationalism. The unknowns are—how fast, how long, how far in public attitudes and especially in public policies this shift will go. Compared with earlier periods of difficulty in the relationship, the duration and depth of today's change of mood is already significant; indeed, to the point where, as will be seen, it is now officially acknowledged to be a major consideration in Canadian foreign policy.

Even with this change, Canadian attitudes toward the American presence follow a complex pattern of cleavage. Geographically, critical concern is sharpest in metropolitan Ontario and least noticeable in the economically "have-not" Atlantic provinces. British Columbia and the Prairie Provinces have customarily been less nationalistic than Ontario. While some recent polls found a more intense nationalism in British Columbia, the heightened concern about the American presence in these areas, particularly in the cities and their academic communities, is dissipated by the endemic suspicion of the Toronto-Ottawa axis that still pervades the vast region from Winnipeg west and which is powerfully fueled today by Alberta energy.

Quebec, of course, has its very special brand of French-Canadian nationalism. The grievances it has with the rest of Canada, along with the province's protective cultural and linguistic insulation and its acute need for developmental assistance, make the American presence a low-priority concern which, at least for the moment, can largely be left to *les Anglais* to worry about in their own bailiwicks.

Explicit, emphatic concern that Canada is about to lose—if, indeed, it has not already lost—its national integrity to the American presence has centered, politically, in the New Democratic Party. The N.D.P.'s socialistic ideology is regarded by its most militant nationalists as not only desirable economic policy, but also as the only practicable way to "buy back" Canada's resources and industries through a program of nationalization.

The two major political parties in the Parliament, the Liberals and the Progressive Conservatives, have been less preoccupied with the American presence. But as Mitchell Sharp's 1972 article on the United States relationship revealed, and as was further witnessed by the Trudeau Government's 1973 post-election strengthening of its proposals for the regulation of foreign direct investment, official circles are clearly becoming more responsive to what is perceived as a mounting public desire for less continentalism, while being careful to stop short of precipitating a late twentieth-century "no truck or trade with the Yankees" imbroglio.

Although Mr. Trudeau proposed in his campaign that at least 50 percent Canadian ownership be required in new resource enterprises, nationalism and the United States relationship figured almost not at all in the 1974 federal election. The election was precipitated by the N.D.P. joining the Conservatives to defeat the Government's budget, and the ensuing campaign was dominated by domestic economic issues. The unexpected result of a strong majority for the Trudeau Government, coupled with serious losses for the N.D.P. as well as the Conservatives, particularly in Ontario, apparently reflected far more dissatisfaction than was generally appreciated with minority government and especially with the N.D.P. as the policy broker in a deadlocked Parliament.

The absence of nationalism in the campaign probably had little significance beyond the fortunate fact that neither of the two main parties saw any advantage in it as an issue. We do well, however, not to mistake a nonissue for a nonconcern. The 1974 election was significant, however, in removing the N.D.P. as the "swing man" in Parliament; its tactical power to press ideological nationalism on either the Government or the opposition is gone at least for some years.

The overall nationalistic trend of the early 1970s is significantly confirmed by the fact that Ottawa's move toward more overt nationalism in public policy was closely paralleled and even foreshadowed by a pronounced shift in this direction in the heartland province—Ontario. The province's Conservative Premier, William Davis, early preempted from the Liberals, and even the N.D.P., the emerging political appeal of a more nationalistic stance. Following several prominent take-overs in 1970 of Canadian publishing houses by American firms, the Ontario Royal Commission on Book Publishing was created to make an urgent, extensive examination of this culturally strategic industry. At the same time, an Interdepartmental Task Force of the provincial government addressed itself to the growing public concern over foreign investment. In 1971 the task force recommended a policy of "moderate economic nationalism." The presumed political appeal of such a position became unmistakable when the Ontario Legislative Assembly followed suit with its own Select Committee on Economic and Cultural Nationalism. The committee has lived up to its rubric with recommendations for Canadianization of foreign-controlled firms and its recent proposals to restrict land purchases by foreigners.

The step-by-step development of the shift in Canadian attitudes over the past twenty years toward a more self-conscious nationalism attracted little attention in the United States. A measure of insight into its progressive intensity is essential, however, if Americans are to understand that they are inescapably dramatis personae in an ongoing Canadian drama, and not merely spectators to a passing scene. Broadly viewed, the period 1939-64 was probably the most harmonious quarter century in the history of the relationship. World War II brought an alliance of the two countries that drew them closer together in both public policy and private activity and attitudes than anyone, expect the early annexationists, had ever dared dream. Indeed, one of Canada's foremost doomsayers, George Grant, in his eloquent *Lament for A Nation*, dates the demise of an independent Canada from this period because "after 1940, the ruling class found its center of gravity in the United States." [2]

Thereafter, of course, the peace was followed by the Cold War with what seemed to most observers in Canada as well as the United States to be the first external security threat to North America in modern times. The threat was perceived as inescapably common to both countries, one which could only be countered by the closest military collaboration in an unprecedented peacetime alliance.

During this period of "continentalism" in new defense arrangements, there was a rapid expansion of the American cultural and economic presence. American publications and broadcasting became overwhelmingly dominant in the mass media, and American direct investment, freshly stimulated by Labrador iron and Alberta oil and gas, became so pervasive in Canada that it could not long go unnoticed and unresented. And yet, however the shared fault in sensitivity and foresight is allotted, it needs remembering, perhaps for the unforeseeable future as well as the unforeseen past, that this burgeoning multiformed American presence was not imposed on a reluctant Canada. In the late 1950s, the well-nigh unanimous acceptance by Canadians, including such old-fashioned nationalists as then Prime Minister John Diefenbaker, that the defense alliance was a Canadian as well as an American national necessity, unquestionably fortified the unexamined assumption of Americans that continentalism in various areas was a mutually shared objective.

As late as 1965, a study sponsored by President Lyndon Johnson and Prime Minister Lester Pearson and carried out by two eminent diplomatists, Ambassadors Livingston Merchant and Arnold Heeney, portrayed the relationship as a functioning, expanding partnership. In point of fact, from 1965 on, the spin-off concerns from the Vietnam war as well as more fundamental worries about the spreading American presence caused "partnership," as a rhetorical concept of the relationship, to be progressively eschewed in Canada. The Merchant-Heeney Report would have been more prescient as to today's relationship if its rhetoric had been attuned to realities which the two ambassadors noted but did not foresee as barriers to the growing partnership they envisaged: "The present preoccupations of . . . Canadians . . . relate primarily to . . . the massive influence of American cultural expression upon Canadian life [and] the extent of American ownership of Canadian industry and resources."

Hindsight now requires us to know that such Canadian preoccupations had already reached a level that within five years would bring Canadian nationalism to the fore as a major, if still officially muted, factor in the reorientation of Canadian foreign policies. "Diversification" became a primary aim in her foreign relations, i.e., less dependence on the United States and official rhetoric increasingly featured assertions of national interest and independence. Canada's determination to seek a more independent relationship with the United States was implicitly forecast in the Trudeau Government's White Papers, *Foreign Policy for Canadians* (1970), and *Defence for the 70s* (1971). In October 1972, the new policy orientation was explicitly spelled out by Mitchell Sharp, then Minister for External Affairs, in his authoritative article, "Canada-United States Relations: Options for the Future."

There could hardly be a more responsible recognition of mounting nationalistic concerns about the American presence than the Minister's candid statement that in today's Canada

> there has been a growing and widely felt concern about the extent of economic, military and cultural dependence on the United States, and the implications for Canadian independence. . . . In the past, Canadians have generally supported an easy-going, pragmatic approach to our relations with the United States in the belief that Canada's separate national existence and development were fully compatible with an unfolding, increasingly close economic, cultural and military relationship between the two countries. Many Canadians no longer accept this view.[3]

If, as a well-known Canadian academic has said, "Mr. Trudeau is easily the least anti-American leader in Canadian history,"[4] the carefully chosen words of his foreign-affairs spokesman, written prior to the political trauma of the October 1972 election, are friendly proof positive, as Mr. Sharp says, that in these matters "public attitudes in Canada . . . have changed." This unusually candid warning about the shift in Canadian attitudes attracted little notice by the American public. Even in business circles, where the change is beginning to be noticed, there has been a tendency to discount it compared with the reassurance taken from the words of the Canadian broadcast journalist, Mr. Sinclair, whose praise of American generosity has been widely rebroadcast in the United States with commerical sponsorship.

Ultimately behind all Canadian nationalism there is the kind of spiritual imperative recently portrayed by the Canadian writer, Margaret Atwood:

> The central symbol for Canada . . . based on numerous instances of its occurrence in both English and French

Canadian literature—is undoubtedly Survival, *la Survivance* ... For French Canada after the English took over it became cultural survival, hanging on as a people, retaining a religion and a language under an alien government. And in English Canada now while the Americans are taking over it is acquiring a similar meaning.

— the main idea is ... hanging on, staying alive. Canadians are forever taking the national pulse ... the aim is not to see whether the patient will live well but simply whether he will live at all. Our central idea is one which generates ... an almost intolerable anxiety.

A preoccupation with one's survival is necessarily also a preoccupation with the obstacles to that survival.[5]

And if the ubiquitous American presence is that obstacle, it is also true, as Canadian scholars have testified, that without this presence Canada might well have had neither the will nor the means to achieve survival. The paradox as well as the preoccupation remain; in today's parlance this is the great Canadian hang-up.

Notes

1. *Capitalism and the National Question in Canada,* Gary Teeple, Editor (Toronto: The University of Toronto Press, 1972), pp. X-XV and 113.
2. George Grant, *Lament For A Nation* (Toronto: McClelland & Stewart, 1965), p. 10.
3. Mitchell Sharp, "Canadian-U.S. Relations: Options for the Future," *International Perspectives* (Autumn 1972), p. 2.
4. James Eayrs, *The Toronto Star*, February 3, 1970.
5. Margaret Atwood, *Survival* (Toronto: House of Anansi Press, Limited, 1972), pp. 32-33.

CHAPTER 6

Cultural Nationalism: Precepts and Policies

Assuming greater national foresight is possible from knowledge of another country's preoccupations, it is unfortunate that, except for a handful of experts, most Americans were unaware of the rising tide of Canadian nationalistic concerns as exhibited over a score of years in the reports of a dozen or more royal commissions and other official inquiries. Only one of the inquiries was explicitly charged with investigating the Canada-U.S. relationship, but the impact of the United States being what it is in Canadian life none could ignore the "American fact," and in several instances it was the central focus. Precepts laid down by these inquiries often foretold the direction of government policies.

Cultural Nationalism
Canada's cultural nationalism, the forerunner of today's "new nationalism," dates at least from the 1951 *Report of the Royal Commission on National Development in the Arts, Letters and Sciences*. The subject, broadly conceived as it was, lent itself to the unabashed, if still heavily British Canadianism of the commission's distinguished Chairman, Vincent

Massey. While couched in a genteel style, the Report sternly summoned Canadians to a more positive concern for their distinctive cultural identity and to a lesser leaning, individually and institutionally, on things American. While gracefully acknowledging benefits gained from the United States, the report focused its main concern on the other side of the coin:

> In this preliminary stock-taking of Canadian cultural life it may be fair to inquire whether we have gained a little too much. . . . Our use of American institutions or our lazy, even abject, imitation of them has caused an uncritical acceptance of ideas and assumptions which are alien to our tradition. . . . It cannot be denied, however, that a vast and disproportionate amount of material coming from a single alien source may stifle rather than stimulate our own creative effort; and passively accepted without any critical standard of comparison, this may weaken critical faculties.

Adjuring Canadians to accept "the paramount importance of strengthening those institutions on which our national morale and national integrity depend," the Massey Report urged, among other things, the exercise of "a strict control over all television stations in Canada in order . . . to encourage Canadian content."

This prescription for Canadian TV broadcasting (following a precept urged on radio by a Royal Commission in 1929), became a national, if not a household, remedy which ever since has been persistently endorsed by investigatorial and regulatory bodies, without, as has often been noted by critics, either killing or curing the patient. As recently as March 1973, Canadian TV was diagnosed in *Maclean's Magazine*, a leading voice of today's nationalism, as suffering from a chronic case of governmentally induced boredom.

The landmark importance and continued impact of the Massey prescription is witnessed by the Report's approving citation (twice noted) by the Minister of External Affairs in his 1972 analysis of the Canada-United States relationship:

"The Massey Commission judged in 1951 that money spent on cultural defences was, in the end, no less important than money spent on defence so-called. In the eyes of most Canadians, this remains a valid judgment." [1]

Broadcasting's Mandate

Five years after the Massey Report, radio and television were singled out for concentrated attention by a royal Commission on Broadcasting under the chairmanship of Robert M. Fowler, a respected business figure and one of Canada's best-informed citizens on Canada-United States relations. The 1957 Fowler Report paid its respect to the Janus-faced dilemma noted by Massey: "No other country is similarly helped and embarrassed by the close proximity of the United States." But by this time Canadian concern was far more portentously expressed:

> . . . as a nation we cannot accept, in these powerful and persuasive media, the natural and complete flow of another nation's culture without danger to our national identity. Can we resist the tidal wave of American cultural activity? Can we retain a Canadian identity, art and culture—a Canadian nationhood? [2]

The Report was prophetic in emphasizing the difficulties involved in finding satisfactory answers to such questions, particularly in the face of indisputable evidence that the Canadian audience preferred American TV productions. On the private versus the public issue, the Commission "bit the bullet," concluding unequivocally that there was no alternative for Canada but "governmental control and regulation of broadcasting," itself a requisite for giving reality to the precepts of nationalism in Canadian broadcasting. The ensuing Broadcasting Act of 1958 established a board of Broadcast Governors empowered "to control the character of any and all programmes broadcast by any stations in Canada" and "to promote and ensure the greater use of Canadian talent by stations in Canada." Subsequently, several full-scale studies of the industry, including a second one chaired by Robert M.

Fowler in 1965, and more recently the 1970 Special Senate Committee on Mass Media, and the revised Broadcast Acts of 1966 and 1968, have uniformly reaffirmed an overtly nationalistic mission for Canadian broadcasting.

Toward this end, today's Broadcast Act calls for a "Canadian broadcasting system owned and controlled by Canadians so as to safeguard, enrich, and strengthen the cultural, political, social and economic fabric of Canada ... using predominantly Canadian creative and other resources ... the national broadcasting service should contribute to the development of national unity and provide for a continuing expression of Canadian identity." The system commands a strong national consensus in support of its mandate to advance cultural nationalism as an essential element of Canadian nationhood. But it also has great problems.

The Canadian broadcasting system involves a complex, competing mixture of public and private ownership; it must transcend the bilingual-bicultural polarization of Canadian society; it serves one of the largest, most sparsely settled national domains on earth, and, above all, in carrying out its mandate it is engaged in an inescapable, ceaseless competition with the powerful American broadcasting industry. With this in mind, it is not surprising that the agency charged with this Herculean mission, the Canadian Radio-Television Commission (C.R.-T.C.), has repeatedly and forthrightly expressed concern about the survival of the system.

Foreign ownershiphof Canadian stations is no longer a significant problem, but, as noted, American programs continue to be preferred by most Canadian viewers and with the coming of cable TV this problem has become worse. Earlier Canadian content requirements aimed at keeping Canadians from being, as the C.R.-T.C. Chairman has said, "a minority voice in their own country" provoked extensive and sterile controversy, particularly with private broadcasters, and also to some extent the public-owned C.B.C., argued that unduly rigid Canadian content requirements were self-defeating because they simply turned many Canadians into habitual viewers of the transborder broadcasts of American stations, resulting in a net audience loss to Canadian broadcasters.

The C.R.-T.C., with a tenacity of purpose and a flexibility of approach that seem to match its remarkable candor as a regulatory agency, has kept the critical Canadian content .question under constant review. In 1975 the basic Canadian content rule required a minimum of 60 percent Canadian general content in television over the program day for both CBC and the private broadcasters, but in evening prime time hours CBC must have 60 percent Canadian programs and the private licensees 50 percent Canadian content. On A.M. radio stations, 30 percent of the recorded music must be Canadian. Cable companies must give preference to available Canadian channels over U.S. channels. The C.R.-T.C. has also proposed that by 1978 all television commercials broadcast in Canada should have a minimum of 80 percent Canadian production, and as of October 1975, all recorded commercial messages on radio were to be produced and recorded in Canada.[3]

The C.R.-T.C. has also tried creating incentives for broadcasters to produce higher quality programs as the most promising, perhaps the only, hope to counter the American TV presence. In 1972, a somewhat flexible approach for meeting the Canadian content requirement was introduced: coproductions of Canadian and foreign producers could qualify as Canadian, provided "50% or more of the total cost of the programme or programmes is spent in Canada on Canadian participation." Preference is given co-productions with Commonwealth or French language countries, for which the required cost of "Canadian participation" ranges from a high of 30 percent down to 10 percent, depending on the number of programs involved.[4] Experience will reveal whether the industry, and particularly the foreign producers, will be sufficiently attracted to the coproduction of such "Special Category Programmes" to raise significantly the attraction of Canadian TV by producing more high-budget programs. There is no prospect, however, that the search for less "American content" in Canadian TV will ever be pursued without restrictive regulation. As the Vice-Chairman of the C.R.-T.C., Harry J. Boyle, realistically told an American audience:

... Canada is a country which exists by reason of communications ... deliberately set up to maintain an east-west flow through our land mass and to resist the normal north-south erosion. ... The whole thing is a challenge ... to develop the vitality and energy within our own nation which will compete rather than live behind artificial restrictions. But there will be certain restrictions because all nations—including yourself, the most powerful nation—take measures to protect fundamentals when any facet of their nationhood is threatened.[5]

In fields such as broadcasting and publishing, the policy-maker quickly discovers how seamless is the line dividing cultural and economic nationalism. Advertising, as will be seen, has provided the principal battleground over the publication of American controlled magazines in Canada and it is now likewise the target of nationalistic regulation in United States-Canada broadcasting relations. The deletion of United States advertisements from American programs on Canadian cable stations has been supported by the C.R.-T.C. and upheld in the lower courts. In over-the-air advertising the Special Committee of the Canadian Senate on Mass Media led the way in 1970 with what then seemed the somewhat unrealistic recommendation that the provision of the Income Tax Law prohibiting the deduction as business expenditures of advertising in foreign-owned magazines be extended to cover advertising expenditures by Canadian firms on American stations broadcasting into Canada, an expenditure currently estimated at some 20 million dollars annually. In January 1975, however, the Trudeau Government decided to parallel its announced intention to move against the Canadian editions of *Time* and *Reader's Digest* with similar treatment for Canadian advertising broadcast on American stations, not to come into effect, however, "until sufficient advertising time is available on Canadian stations to satisfy Canadian needs adequately." [6] A notable expression, indeed, of *Realpolitik* in cultural and/or economic nationalism.

National Reading Fare

In 1961 the reading fare of Canadians received the attention of a Royal Commission. Once again the way had been blazed by the Massey Report's singling out of Canada's periodical press as "our closest approximation to a national literature." Mr. Massey's Commission had paid tribute to Canadian magazines for managing "to survive and even to flourish although American periodicals [in 1951] outsell them by more than two to one in their own Canadian market" and for "remaining resolutely Canadian" despite problems "that symbolize many of the problems of Canada as a nation and Canadians as a people." [7] Ten years later, the mounting competition of American magazines and the overpowering attraction of television for the advertising dollar created a climate of crisis in the Canadian periodicals industry. A Royal Commission on Publications, chaired by M. G. O'Leary, undertook an inquiry which discovered that however serious the plight of Canadian periodicals, there was a vast chasm between concern and effective policy in cultural nationalism.

The O'Leary Commission found the familiar scenario in which the American presence was the heavy and, as in broadcasting, where the gravamen was that "only a truly Canadian printing press, one with the 'feel' of Canada and directly responsible to Canada, can give us the critical analysis, the informed discourse and dialogue which are indispensable in a sovereign society." [8] The Commission's proclaimed "sole purpose . . . to find a way to guarantee for Canadians their own communications media" led again, as in broadcasting, to the conclusion that drastic governmental action was necessary "to insure a climate of competition in which Canadian publications . . . shall have a chance to survive." [9] The O'Leary Commission reported "three out of every four magazines read by Canadians . . [are] imported from the United States. *Time* and *Reader's Digest* [get] over 40 per cent of the total spent on magazines in Canada." Most serious of all, the locally published Canadian editions of these two bestsellers, and the other American imports, were alleged to be depriving indigenous Canadian publications of a fair share of what was left in advertising revenue after television got a progressively larger share of it. There obviously was no certainty that this advertising could be shifted from American to Canadian magazines, and the argument was pressed that the net result would simply be to transfer more of it from magazines to television. With few alternatives open to it, the O'Leary Commission recommended governmental action to divert such revenues to homegrown periodicals by (1) denying income-tax deductibility for Canadian advertising in foreign periodicals "wherever printed" and (2) denying import into Canada of periodicals containing advertising directed at the Canadian market.

The O'Leary Commission's recommendations attracted relatively little public attention in the United States; they did, however, ignite a widespread controversy in Canada. The diplomatic difficulties which ensued aroused the White House, raised fears in the Canadian cabinet for the Auto Pact negotiations, and produced slightly surrealist visions of the consequences for United States-Canada relations generally if the displeasure of *Time*'s Henry Luce was not assuaged.

In any event, and for a mixed bag of reasons, in mid-1965, after nearly four years of domestic debate and transborder controversy, the O'Leary Report's two principal recommendations became the basis of legislation: (1) the customs law was amended to bar imported periodicals containing advertising directed at the Canadian market; (2) foreign ownership of periodical and newspaper publishing in Canada was dealt with in the Income Tax Act by requiring 75 percent Canadian ownership of such publications before advertising in them qualifies as a deductible business expense of the advertiser. But the law's exemptions attracted more attention than the ownership requirement itself. Without being specifically named, the Canadian editions of *Time* and *Reader's Digest* became the beneficiaries of a "grandfather clause" in the new law which, based on their previous publication in Canada, exempted them from the new Canadian ownership requirement. Thereafter, with these two notable exceptions, Canadian periodicals and newspapers became off-limits to American control.

If the spreading American presence and its counterpart, a rising nationalism, had peaked in the mid-1960s, the *Time* and *Reader's Digest* contretemps would presumably by now have passed into the calm harbor of history. Their widespread popularity with Canadian readers might well have won them a fully accepted place in the Canadian scheme of things. But in fact neither the American presence nor Canadian nationalism had crested and as both mounted in the late 1960s and early 1970s, the exemption accorded this prominent American presence by the Canadian Income Tax Act provided a continuing target for nationalistic concerns. Within five years the special status of the two magazines was denounced by parliamentary committees of both the House of Commons and the Senate with strong recommendations that their exempt status be cancelled.

In 1970, the Standing Committee on External Affairs and National Defence of the House of Commons devoted its "principal effort . . . to a basic examination of relations with the United States." This somewhat unusual undertaking ranged comprehensively across the spectrum of the American presence in Canada. The Committee's Report, adopted 11 to 1, makes numerous recommendations, mostly with a pronounced nationalistic orientation, including specifically "that the privileged position of *Time* and *Reader's Digest* should be terminated and their exemption from the special provisions of the Income Tax Act relating to foreign-owned periodicals should be eliminated."

Also in 1970, the Special Committee of the Canadian Senate on Mass Media (Keith Davey, Chairman), whose vivid picture of the contemporary American magazine presence was mentioned earlier, focused its recommendations on the same target. The Committee went into the pros and cons of the special status accorded *Time* and *Reader's Digest*. On the pro side, particularly on issues directly relevant to nationalistic concerns, the Report was frank to concede that "There is no question that both magazines have been good corporate citizens," noting specifically that the shares of *Reader's Digest* "are traded on the open market, and about 30 percent of the stock in the subsidiary is now held by Canadians. . . . The

Company has about 450 employees in Canada, including an editorial staff almost as large as that of MacLean's . . . and four of its six directors are Canadian." *Time,* in turn, was generally acknowledged to be doing a responsible, first-rate job of reporting the Canadian as well as the world scene; indeed, no less an authority on the subject than Senator Gratton O'Leary, the chairman of the 1961 Royal Commission on Publications, testified before the Davey Committee that the quality of Canadian magazines had declined to the point where "Were I making my report today I would not have been so concerned for those magazines. . . . I am not sure that *Time* magazine today is not the best Canadian magazine we have." [10]

Despite such a testimonial and the apparent readiness of the major Canadian magazines to live with the status quo, Senator Davey and his colleagues on the Special Senate Committee voted fourteen to one to "recommend that the exemption now granted *Time* and *Reader's Digest* under . . . the Income Tax Act be repealed, and the sooner the better." The Committee summed up its position thus:

> Somehow or other, we've arrived in the peculiarly Canadian position where our most successful magazines are American magazines, and we're moving inexorably toward the day when they'll be the *only* magazines we have. This may make sense in terms of economics; on every other basis it's intolerable.

The explanation given by the Committee for its verdict of "good but guilty" is especially revealing of the syndrome against which such issues are perceived in Canada today:

> We believe that creeping continentalism has proceeded far enough in this country. We believe the present situation of the magazine industry is a perfect example of the dangers of an unexamined acceptance of foreign investment. That is our feeling, and we believe it is shared by most Canadians. . . . Somewhere, somehow, in all our national deliberations, the line must be drawn between logic and love. . . . The consumer magazine seg-

ment of the industry is by far the most important seg-
ment in terms of our cultural survival. . . . Whatever the
admen say, whatever the economists say, this is a situation we should no longer tolerate.[11]

Time and *Reader's Digest* today command a combined
unrivalled readership upwards of two million, even as inescapably they have also served as a kind of hostage to Canada's
cultural nationalism, or, perhaps more realistically, as hostage
to the economic fortunes of the Canadian periodical industry.
In 1972 these fortunes turned temporarily favorable to the
point where the *Financial Times of Canada* suggested that
the threat to the industry featured by the "much-ballyhooed"
O'Leary and Davey investigations "now appears to have been
largely illusory." [12]
However illusory "the threat" may have been, the concern
in nationalistic circles did not abate. By the fall of 1974 the
status of the two magazines (there was some support for
viewing *Reader's Digest* more favorably) was once again being
sharply debated by a Canadian Cabinet. In October, *Saturday
Night*, Canada's oldest magazine suspended publication
because of financial difficulties. On January 23, 1975, the
Trudeau Government announced its decision to bring in
legislation withdrawing the 1965 exemptions, thereby making
advertising expenditures in both magazines nondeductible
effective January 1, 1976. The action and the efforts of the two
magazines to prevent it stirred considerable controversy that
continues but, unlike the situation in the early 1960s American diplomacy was little, if at all, involved. If, as seems
certain, Parliament approves the withdrawal of the 1965 exemptions, one or both of the two magazines may seek to remain by meeting the requirements for 75% Canadian equity
control and a substantially greater Canadian content. Whatever the outcome for *Time* and *Reader's Digest* and for *Mac-
Lean's Magazine* seeking to be Canada's first indigenous
newsmagazine, the action could be a portentous victory for
Canadian nationalism. Only future Canadians will know
whether it created a stronger nation and better society.

Books

Coincidentally or otherwise, 1970 was the year when the so-called new nationalism began to meet head-on the perplexities that in every area of public affairs stand between precept and governmental policy. It was the year of the Government's White Paper, *Foreign Policy for Canadians*, and the prelude to its 1971 sequel, the White Paper, *Defence in the 70s*, both noticeably more nationalistic in rhetoric and more cautious in their approach to the Canada-United States relationship than official utterances only five to ten years earlier. Likewise, as noted above, it was also the year of two major parliamentary inquiries, both largely devoted to nationalistic concerns. Perhaps most significantly of all, it was in the spring of 1970 that the Trudeau government gave its then Minister of Revenue, Herb Gray, as stated in the Foreword of the Gray Report, "the responsibility of bringing forward proposals on foreign investment policy for the consideration of the government."

It was in this 1970 climate that worries about the American cultural presence became acute when several major publishing enterprises, including Canada's oldest and largest firm, The Ryerson Press, became American take-overs. "The alarm," as the reaction was characterized in the governmental newsletter, *Canada Today*, produced action, as well as strong reactions, in both the book industry itself and in governmental circles.

The Special Senate Committee on Mass Media (the Davey Report), while expressing regret at not being able, because of time, to deal with book publishing, nevertheless registered the strong belief that "it is urgently necessary to consider whether this industry—like banking, uranium, broadcasting, and newspaper and periodical publishing—should not be declared off-limits to foreign takeovers." [13]

Presumably by coincidence but manifestly out of a shared alarm, the Davey Report's stricture came at the same time, December 1970, that the government of Ontario created a Royal Commission on the publishing industry. Although initiated on the provincial level, the two-year inquiry inevitably addressed itself to the national scene as well since Ontario is the heartland of English publishing in Canada. The Report, published in 1973, is beyond doubt the most comprehensive study ever done, in the words of the Commission's mandate, of "the economic, cultural, social or other consequences for the people of Ontario and of Canada of the substantial ownership of publishing firms by . . non-Canadians." [14] More fundamentally, it is also an insightful, balanced approach to certain of the dilemmas inherent in the concept of cultural nationalism.

The Report of the Ontario Royal Commission on Book Publishing is reassuring witness that cultural nationalism in Canada need not lose its way for want of a penetrating, responsible analysis of what is at issue. As a penetrating examination of the Canadian book-publishing scene, its judgments have value for the entire international community. All too often man's proudest product, human culture itself, and its contribution to a healthy nationalism get lost in pyrotechnics when the two are required to serve the political purposes of a nation-state. Few contemporary societies have generated comparable insight into the pros and cons of cultural nationalism to that contained in this passage quoted by the Ontario Royal Commission "with special enthusiasm" from a Report of the Economic Council of Canada:

> . . . most Canadians desire for their country (full account being taken of its fundamentally bilingual and bicultural character) a strong and distinctive cultural identity. We have further assumed that, for this, most Canadians would be willing to pay some as yet undetermined economic price. . . . The cultural identity sought should as quickly as possible become a sturdy and viable entity, capable of holding its own in the world without shame or inordinate special protection. . . . To reduce the matter to a concrete example, any decision-maker responsible for foisting upon Canadian students a third-rate textbook simply because it is written and produced in Canada should consider himself overdue for an interview with his conscience and a careful contemplation of the long forward shadow cast by the quality of education. . . . Low-grade cultural parochialism does no serv-

ice to the cause of a durable and creative Canadian nationalism—quite the contrary. . . . It is particularly important that the relevance of cultural goals in a policy-planning situation should not be used as a smoke screen behind which material interests and conflicts between private and social interests are allowed to shelter unexamined.[15]

Being committed to such a philosophy, it is not surprising that the Commission rejected import prohibitions and quotas on books, "as was seriously recommended to us, . . . The intellectual censorship inherent in such restrictions would be rejected by Canadians, as it would be by any other free society."

Likewise, even though rejecting counsel from the other end of the remedial spectrum that "ownership of publishing houses in Canada is of no cultural consequence," the Commission found little attraction in the argument favoring "enforced Canadianization of foreign-owned publishers" on the ground (as suggested above in the Davey Report) that book publishing was a part of the communications industry and like radio, television, newspapers, and magazines "should be brought under equally stringent control." Having eschewed such negative policy measures and the "anti-American bias [that] sometimes underlies the enthusiasm for emasculating the subsidiaries," the Commission went on to make the case for positive measure to promote Canadian ownership on two principal counts: (1) to provide Canadian schools, particularly below the university level, with first-rate texts based primarily on the Canadian experience and (2) to assure the nation a "residual Canadian ownership" in the industry in order to keep the foreign subsidiaries on their mettle. The Canadian market would then not be left simply to "become part of the run-on continental market" with no competitive incentive to keep American publishers interested in original Canadian books as their subsidiaries in Canada must now be, at least to a significant degree.

The Commission also based its great concern for the protection of such residual Canadian ownership in the book-publishing industry on a consideration that tends to be neglected:

> ... who—other than Canadian-owned publishers—will foster the books that will report the discussions of ownership that gave rise to this Commission, say, or that will spearhead whatever campaigns may be mounted in the future on behalf of Canadian cultural or economic nationalism? It is not necessary to be an ultra-nationalist to say that this country must always possess a publishing facility which is prepared to present, and promote if necessary, every point of view on such basic issues. A short catalogue of some of the more outspoken works on behalf of Canadian national interests published in recent years will demonstrate the point: *The New Romans; What Culture? What Heritage?; The Struggle for Canadian Universities; Gordon to Watkins to You; Close the Forty-Ninth Parallel, etc.; Read Canadian; An Independent Foreign Policy for Canada?; An Independent Foreign Policy for Canada?; The Wretched of Canada.* Not one of these books was issued by a foreign-owned publishing house. How many of them would have been published had there been no Canadian-owned publishers? How many of them would have been left unwritten, in such circumstances? [16]

The mere existence of such a literature in Canada (the list could readily be doubled) is understandably if unfortunately all but unknown in the United States. History and reason support the judgment that Canadian nationalism must *always* have the opportunity for being vented, if it is not be become explosively paranoid. Inescapably this depends on residual Canadian ownership in the book industry of the nation. The mass media reach more people but compared with books, their impact is usually short-lived and rootless; indeed, more often than not, their presentations derive from books.

The Commission, born in the crisis climate of the 1970 take-overs, moved swiftly from concern to action. Three months to the day after its creation, it recommended that the government of Ontario arrange a rather dramatic emergency loan of about 1 million dollars, on very soft terms, to prevent the bankruptcy or possible sale to American interests of McClelland and Stewart, a major Canadian-owned house, presided over by Jack McClelland, a leading nationalist. The government acted favorably on this and another recommended rescue (an additional 850,000 dollars is reported to have been made available to other publishers as of March 1973) with the result that capital assistance to publishers is now Ontario government policy. In recommending the capital-loans assistance program, the commission initially laid down what it termed "an important corollary," namely, that the government should announce that any further sales of Canadian-owned book publishers to nonresidents "will be considered contrary to the public interest." Subsequently the Commission, perhaps influenced by Ottawa's intervening proposals for the creation of a Federal agency to screen take-overs and new foreign investment, modified its position from one of flat opposition to future take-overs to one of requiring prior approval by a screening agency, the proposed Ontario Book Publishing Board, for additional book-publishing enterprises as well as take-overs of existing firms by nonresidents. As of 1975 this recommendation had not been enacted.

Whatever form governmental implementation of these recommendations may take, it now seems probable that the commission is correct in its observation that a "voluntary trend in the direction of Canadianization of ownership," or at least in avoiding further Americanization, is now developing in this industry. A significant straw in this rising wind was the action in 1972 of McGraw-Hill, Inc., of New York, to introduce Canadian ownership in its Canadian subsidiary, McGraw-Hill Ryerson Ltd., by a public offering in Canada of about 30 percent of the subsidiary's outstanding stock.

There are other significant indications that public policy related to reading fare is pointing toward greater Canadianization in various ways:

(1) The commission's strong stand against "the further erosion of Canadian ownership" in the wholesale dis-

tribution of periodicals and mass-market paperbacks which was implemented by legislation in *The Paperback and Periodical Distributors Act, 1971*. A position that was subsequently strengthened with recommendations aimed at reducing the dominance of certain United States-owned wholesalers, particularly in the metropolitan Toronto area, and at preventing new ownership of retail news dealers and booksellers by nonresidents.

(2) The commission's recommendation that the various new programs aimed at strengthening the Canadianization of the industry, budgeted minimally at one million dollars annually, should be mainly financed by rescinding the existing exemption now given periodicals from the province's 5 percent sales tax, a recommendation frankly keyed to the dominant American presence (upward of 90 percent for this purpose) in Ontario's periodical market: "We do not propose to offer new solutions to the cultural threat posed by imported periodical literature, but we do take the position that its continued expansion should not be sheltered in this province by special tax concessions of any kind." Any slight adverse effect on culturally important Canadian magazines would be taken care of by "a special program of support."

(3) Most significantly of all, the main concern of the Commission was to protect and promote in all ways consistent with educational quality the "Canadian content" of reading materials used in the elementary and secondary schools. Both by reason of its critical front-line position in the cause of cultural nationalism, and because unlike the general trade and university book markets it is susceptible to public financing pressures and preferential policies, schoolbook publishing was given priority attention. Specifically, the Commission came down firmly behind retaining and strengthening Ontario's long-standing Canada preference policy and its "circular 14" of approved schoolbooks as to authorship and manufacture.

As in all countries, the schoolroom is inevitably an early and prime target of nationalism; as such it is an area of a nation's life that merits much more attention than it customarily gets from those seeking a better understanding of the fashioning forces behind national policies. Education being a provincial responsibility under the Canadian constitution, nationalistic concerns will continue to spark controversy in the provinces in respect to teaching personnel, textbooks, and curriculum.

Cultural nationalism often finds itself confounded by cultural regionalism. The Ontario Commission discovered this while investigating the possibility of getting other provinces to collaborate with Ontario on a Canadian preference policy for textbooks: "Ontario textbooks can be as foreign as any American or British textbook to a province like Alberta, . . . as was diplomatically pointed out to the Commission on its visit there." Regionalism will often be a limitation on efforts to translate precepts of cultural as well as economic nationalism into nationwide policies.

And yet, with all their significant diversities, the individual but common concerns of the provinces are often instructive as to national concerns and policy directions. For example, Quebec, even with its cultural and linguistic insulation, has developed policies of its own to prevent foreign control of its book industry. All bookstores and publishing houses in Quebec require the provincial government's accreditation which has been contingent upon the enterprise being at least 50 percent owned by a Canadian citizen living in Quebec. The recent acquisition of a Quebec distributing outlet by a Montreal firm in which the large Paris-based publishing house, Hachette-France, owned a substantial minority interest resulted in an outcry in the French-Canadian publishing industry against foreign take-overs. The industry went so far as to petition the Quebec Ministry of Cultural Affairs to reduce the ceiling on foreign ownership in the book business from 50 to 20 percent. This was not done, but the governmental screening process has been tightened to head off any further growth of foreign control in the field, and other measures, such as requiring Quebec schoolboards to buy all their books published in English from Quebec booksellers, make it clear that the province intends to keep control of its reading in Quebec hands.

Ottawa's concern with the American presence in Canada's publishing industry has not produced an inquiry comparable to the Ontario Royal Commission. Ontario's dominant position in English-language publishing assures the province of a major influence on policies for the industry. At the same time, Ottawa's primacy in international matters, its financial assistance to the industry, 5.5 million dollars in 1975, and its commitment to an effective Federal program for screening foreign take-overs and new investment, all portend a more aggressive Federal role in support of a Canadian controlled book industry. The Gray Report was explicit about there being high foreign control in "industries which have considerable cultural impact such as book publishing," and it is likely that future foreign investment in this industry will be faced increasingly with the double hurdle of active concern on the part of both Ottawa and the provinces.

The effectiveness of governmental grants and promotional efforts in aid of Canadian publishing is still to be demonstrated, while the enormous difficulties of an industry based on a relatively small, highly dispersed home market in constant confrontation with the American publsihing industry are readily apparent. Conceivably the problem of squaring cultural nationalism with both the values of a free society and the economic realities of pubishing may present Canada with issues even more complicated and controversial than the dilemmas of economic nationalism.

Indeed, cultural nationalism may be a particularly good barometer for reading the longer-run outlook for Canadian nationalism generally. It tends to be grounded more in emotion and sentiment than is often the case with the conflicting material interests of economic nationalism. It is well, therefore, for Americans to savor the sentiments of fifteen members of the Canadian Senate who, in the Davey Report (1970), avowed their concern over

> . . . the lengthening odds on our cultural survival . . . what is at stake . . . involves the survival of our nationhood. . . .

One of the witnesses who appeared before us warned that "Canada has one decade remaining in which its members have to make up their minds whether they want to remain a distinct political, cultural and geographical nationality." The C.R.T.C.'s [Chairman] Pierre Juneau . . . concurred in this assessment. So do we.[17]

Cultural survival is perhaps the most critical problem our generation of Canadians will have to face, and it may be it can be achieved only by using all the means at our command.[18]

The twenty years between the Massey Report and the Davey Report on Mass Media witnessed a significant rise in the apprehensions and stridency of Canadian cultural nationalism. The cultural impact of the Americanization syndrome is increasingly perceived as the acute malaise of Canadian nationhood. The nationalistic perception of international cultural affairs projected by the Massey Report has now become a national imperative for those Canadians who share the judgment of a prominent Canadian editor, Robert Fulford, that " 'cultural nationalism' is what Canada today is all about." [19] Unusual but convincing "grass-roots" evidence of the scope of this concern was recently provided by the readiness of the Trudeau Government to legislate if necessary (it was not necessary) to bar the presence of American teams and more "imports" in Canadian professional football.[20] Hockey and baseball, yes; football, no, at least not in 1974.

Notes

1. Mitchell Sharp, "Canada-U.S. Relations: Options for the Future," *International Perspectives* (Autumn 1972), p. 19.
2. *Report* of Royal Commission on Broadcasting (Ontario Queen's Printer, 1957), p. 8.
3. Dept. of External Affairs, *Reference Papers*, Vol. 136, June 1974, and C.R.-T.C. Notice of Appearance, Public Hearing October 8, 1974.
4. C.R.-T.C. Public Announcement, Broadcast Regulations, July 20, 1972.

5. Harry J. Boyle, Vice-Chairman, C.R.-T.C., speech in San Francisco, December 29, 1969.

6. *Canada Weekly*, February 12, 1975, reporting statement of Secretary of State J. Hugh Faulkner in House of Commons, January 23, 1975.

7. Quoted in *Mass Media*, Vol. III, p. 211.

8. *Report* of the Royal Commission on Publications, M. G. O'Leary, Chairman, 1961, p. 7.

9. Ibid, p. 93.

10. *Mass Media*, Vol, I, *supra*, pp. 153-168.

11. *Mass Media*, Vol. I, *supra*.

12. *Financial Times of Canada*, April 16, 1973, p. 20.

13. Davey Report, Preface, p. VIII.

14. *Canadian Publishers & Canadian Publishing* (Ontario: Queen's Printer, 1973).

15. *Canadian Publishers & Canadian Publishing*, p. 81, quoting from the Economic Council of Canada's *Report on Intellectual and Industrial Property*, 1971.

16. *Canadian Publishers & Canadian Publishing*, p. 69.

17. Davey Report, p. 11.

18. Ibid, p. 194.

19. Robert Fulford interview, *Glode and Mail*, Toronto, March 16, 1972.

20. *New York Times*, April 11, 1974, p. 43; and *Canada Weekly*, Dept. of External Affairs, April 3, 1974.

CHAPTER 7

Economic Nationalism: A New National Policy?

Economic nationalism in any comprehensive sense would be a more difficult concept to package in a program of coherent Canadian policy than cultural nationalism. The nation's highly regionalized national economy and the necessary accommodation of conflicting economic interests through a federally organized, dominantly decentralized political process all but assures that Canada's economic nationalism will be much more pragmatic than doctrinaire.

Economic nationalism in Canada must also come to terms with the fact that the nation's economic vitality and even its political viability are far more closely tied to the realities of international economics than would ever be compatible with a doctrinaire economic nationalism. Americans with some experience in international commercial policy during the period between the two world wars must also be mindful that there is a threshold problem of semantics. During the period of international economic strife that characterized much of the interwar period, "economic nationalism" became essentially a term connoting a governmentally imposed system of national economic self-sufficiency, in a word, autarchy. In Canada

today, economic nationalism is rarely used in this sense. Its
contemporary use, particularly in academic circles, is a precept
directed at reducing American ownership and control in Canadian industry and natural resources.

Many, perhaps most, of the academics who are committed
to economic nationalism are also outspoken advocates of reducing Canadian protectionism, both to make foreign ownership of Canadian industry less attractive and in order to
stimulate greater productivity, thereby strengthening Canada's competitive position in world markets on which the
nation depends for about 25 percent of its G.N.P.

Canadian protectionism is proudly a lineal descendant of
the 1879 National Policy of John A. MacDonald, the father
and first Prime Minister of Confederation. Except for the
aborted approach at reciprocity with the United States in
1911, an effort that played a major part in Prime Minister
Laurier's political demise, protectionism has been a residual
national policy, essentially a nonissue in the mainstream of
Canadian political life, for nearly a century. In recent years
liberal trade policies have found a widening acceptance as
Canada aggressively sought broader foreign markets, beyond
the Commonwealth, particularly for labor-intensive industrial
products. Similarly, the increasing concern about American
direct investment points, at least theoretically, in the same
direction.

The cause-and-effect relationship between Canadian protectionism and the inflow of American investment has never
been a secret to economists, but the connection with today's
nationalistic concerns has never been put more baldly than by
Michael Bliss, a University of Toronto historian, in writing on
"Canadianizing American Business: The Roots of the Branch
Plant":

> As economists have long recognized and historians long
> ignored, the roots of the branch-plant economic struc-
> ture in North America must clearly be traced to the
> operations of the National Policy of tariff protection. . . .
> The economic nationalism of the late nineteenth cen-
> tury, then, operated and was known to operate to induce

Americans to enter Canada and participate directly in the Canadian economy. Accordingly, the National Policy sowed many of the seeds of our present problem with foreign ownership. . . . From the perspective of the late 1960s it now appears to have been a peculiarly self-defeating kind of economic nationalism. The funny thing about our tariff walls was that we always wanted the enemy to jump over them. Some walls! [1]

There is a small, politically unimportant element on the outer edge of greater trade protectionism whose litany decries liberal trade policies as a mask for American economic exploitation. So long as times are good, or at least as good as they have been in recent years, this view has little prospect of acceptance even in militant nationalistic circles. For example, Walter Gordon, a founder and patron saint of the Committee for an Independent Canada, while finding continentalism and economic integration of the two countries abhorrent, rejects the counsel of these fellow nationalists who would:

> go to another extreme and somehow or other reduce the amount, or the portion of our trade with the United States. . . . it would be unwise for Canada to take action in any overt way which was aimed at diverting a proportion of our trade elsewhere. The fact that we have access . . . to the great American market is a major reason for our affluence and prosperity. . . . We should break up the present relationship of the larger Canadian subsidiaries and their foreign parent corporations. . . . But, let me repeat, we ourselves should not do anything that would disrupt or weaken the trade we now enjoy with our neighbor to the south. [2]

Many economists, of course, would assert that contemporary international economic activity generally involves a closer linkage between trade and foreign investment than Mr. Gordon appears to acknowledge. Certainly as matters stand today, trade and investment are integral parts of the American economic presence in Canada. The Gray Report notes the high proportion of Canada's foreign trade, upward of 40 percent, that is carried on by American subsidiaries; nearly 80 percent of this trade involved transactions of subsidiaries with parent companies and affiliates in the United States.[3] Whatever may be the ultimate course of Canadian policy in dealing with the American trade and investment presences, a realistic understanding of the situation cannot start with the assumption that the two are readily separable, especially not in the largest single trade sector, the automotive industry.

For Canadian nationalists, the American branch plant is the twentieth-century's version of the Trojan horse; American ownership and control of better than half of Canada's most important industries is the enemy within the walls. The American direct investment presence produces more outspoken criticism than the cultural presence, presumably in part at least because of the high percentage of Canadians whose personal preferences in reading and TV strongly favor the American media. On the other hand, the reactions of Canadians in public-opinion surveys, group resolutions, editorials, speeches, articles, books and private talk, are increasingly critical of a more impersonal situation that is pictured as American versus Canadian ownership of things Canadian. Such an adversary view readily calls forth semantic weapons: "imperialism" and "colonialism," familiar battle cries in the Canadian experience.

Although the restriction of foreign investment came to Canada more slowly than to any comparable country, public opinion surveys have shown for some time that close to a majority of Canadians would accept the economic cost of restricting foreign investment. During the past decade, this public attitude became widespread and outspoken. The largest federation of labor unions, the C.L.C., demanded restrictive action, as did the political establishment, e.g., the 1973 annual meeting of the Ontario Liberal Party voted over ten to one "that foreign ownership poses a serious threat to Canada's independence and that Canadian control and ownership is of the highest importance." [4] The centers of militant nationalism, the N.D.P. and the Committee for an Independent Canada, have kept up a drumfire of hot concern and the editorial orientation of such major publications as *The Toronto Star* and *MacLean's Magazine* has been and continues emphatically nationalistic. The search for restrictive policies on foreign ownership became a pressing issue in Canada's public life during the late 1960s, and by 1972 this concern had reached a point of public preoccupation from which there was no exit except through governmental action.

According to the eminent historian Donald Creighton, Canada's contemporary economic nationalism took its rise,in the mid-1950s from the controversy over the way the St. Laurent government (particularly C. D. Howe) pushed the trans-Canada pipeline through Parliament. If so, it was a significant coincidence that the search for a national policy on foreign investment was, so to speak, launched in 1955 by that government's creation of a Royal Commission on Canada's Economic Prospects, under the chairmanship of Walter Gordon, a public-spirited, businessman-accountant who later became the leader of Canada's "new nationalism." As with other Royal Commissions of the period, including Vincent Massey's landmark venture five years earlier on National Development in the Arts, Letters, and Sciences, the Canada-United States relationship, while not specified in the commission's mandate, was a central concern. The Commission was served by a strong staff under the direction of one of Canada's most broadly talented academics (with significant government experience), Douglas V. Le Pan. The Report of the Commission in 1957, as well as a Preliminary Report, rank in scope, penetration, and even eloquence among the very best ever produced by Canada's many Royal Commissions.

The distinguished American economist (a former Canadian), Jacob Viner, found "the general tone of the Report . . . decidedly nationalistic," [5] a judgment called forth in part by the commission's observation that with the growing dominance of American capital in resource and manufacturing industries "our economy will inevitably become more and more integrated with that of the United States. Behind this is the fear that continuing integration might lead to economic domination by the United States and eventually to the loss of our political independence. This fear of domination by the

United States affects to some extent the political climate of life in Canada today [1957]." [6]

Like the inquiries which dealt with the American cultural presence, the Gordon Commission found itself confronted with the classical Canadian dilemma: concerns about independent nationhood were largely hypothetical while benefits from the American presence were real, omnipresent, and all too manifestly enjoyable. The Commission accordingly approached the task of suggesting "reasonable and realistic objectives respecting foreign investment and operations of Canadian subsidiaries of foreign companies . . . aware that it is treading on somewhat treacherous and uncertain ground"—a policy peril that, as will be seen, has not been eliminated, even after two more decades of study and debate.

The Gordon Commission did venture to propose three policy objectives: (1) "more foreign capital in the form of loans rather than equity control"; (2) the association of "Canadian capital and Canadian interests" with foreign investments in resource and manufacturing industries; and (3) "ensure that control of Canadian banks and other financial institutions is retained in Canada." The third objective was underscored as being "most important," an area meriting "stronger action," and one in whose importance "we believe firmly."

How firmly Chairman Gordon believed in this last recommendation was dramatically affirmed a few years later when he and the issue became the center of a *cause célèbre*, the Mercantile Bank case. This take-over controversy raged over four years in the mid-1960s and involved a leading American bank, two aroused governments, and at times a bitterly divided Canadian Cabinet. It resulted in restrictive legislation, extensive coast-to-coast publicity including nearly two hundred editorials, and probably did more than any other recent happening to spread the fear of Americanization throughout Canada.

An American student of the affair, Professor John Fayerweather,[7] judged the substantive issues involved to have been relatively unimportant compared to the national emotion that was aroused. However that may be, and the issue still stirs heated argument in Canada, there can be little doubt that overall the affair powerfully stimulated today's nationalism and helped prepare the way for the restrictive approach to foreign investment that finally surfaced officially in 1972. A classic confrontation between a major American enterprise and Canadian economic nationalism as personified by the then new Minister of Finance, the former Chairman of the Royal Commission on Canada's Economic Prospects, Walter Gordon, the affair helped restore Mr. Gordon's public position after his nearly disastrous experience in seeking to curtail American investment through taxation proposals in his initial budget as Minister of Finance in Lester Pearson's first Cabinet. If Canada's new nationalism was in need of a prominent figure to lead it, the Mercantile Bank controversy cast Walter Gordon for that role. Thereafter he championed the cause of economic nationalism both as an official and later as a founder of the Committee for an Independent Canada.

Although the full story of the affair is a long one with aspects that remain in dispute, the essentials are straightforward and instructive. In 1963, the First National City Bank of New York (Citibank) undertook to establish a subsidiary operation in Canada by acquiring ownership of a relatively minor Canadian enterprise, the Mercantile Bank, which up to that time had been owned by Dutch interests. There was no legal barrier to the transaction, but top-level Canadian officials (Louis Rasminsky, Governor of the Bank of Canada, and Walter Gordon, Minister of Finance) warned against it as being contrary to Canadian wishes. The controversy focused on whether these warnings had been ignored or had come too late. Gordon charged that Citibank closed the deal only *after* he had warned the bank of his opposition and of prospective restrictions. Citibank officials claimed, to the contrary, that the purchase had been agreed upon before they knew of Mr. Gordon's strong opposition. In a subsequent parliamentary proceeding, as will be seen, the American bankers were pressed to explain how they could have been unaware, long before they met with Mr. Gordon, of his previously publicized views and of the mounting concern in Canada on such matters.

In 1965 Minister Gordon moved, as he had earlier threatened, to have Parliament bar the expansion of any bank if more than 25 percent of its stock was owned by non-Canadian interests as, of course, had been the case with the Mercantile as a wholly owned subsidiary of Citibank since September 1963. In 1967, following an election and Gordon's replacement by Mitchell Sharp as Minister of Finance and some strong diplomatic as well as intra-Cabinet exchanges, the Canadian Bank Act was amended to require a minimum of 75 percent Canadian ownership of chartered banks, but with a compromise postponement of the limitation on Mercantile's future expansion to permit Citibank to have five years from December 31, 1967 to comply with the 25 percent foreign-ownership ceiling, a divesting period later extended to 1980.

In January 1967, when the then head of Citibank, James S. Rockefeller and a number of his principal associates, appeared before a committee of the House of Commons to oppose the proposed restrictive legislation, the committee indicated its incredulity that a bank of Citibank's international position had undertaken the acquisition of a Canadian chartered bank without being aware that such a transaction would not be welcomed in Canada and, indeed, would be in direct conflict with the previously publicized position of the Minister of Finance.

The response of Mr. Rockefeller suggests how long ago 1963 was: as to his knowledge of Walter Gordon prior to discussing the matter with him in July 1963, he knew only that he "was an accountant" and was regarded as "a very nice gentleman"; asked whether he had not previously known of Gordon's strong feelings about foreign ownership, he replied:

> No, I certainly did not. . . . Mr. Gordon's attitude was a shock to me; it was such a surprise. Neither was I familiar with the famous book at that time, you know. . . . We did not get this feeling of nationalism, or whatever you want to call it. We consider ourselves friendly neighbors. . . . No, honestly, it did not cross our thoughts. . . . All I can say is that in my daily work I am in touch with executive officers of a great many corporations, many of which have

operations in Canada, and I cannot recall any of them coming in and bemoaning any Canadian problems they had.

Citibank's unawareness of the indigenous American factor in Canadian nationalism was highlighted when one of Mr. Rockefeller's associates, seeking to be helpful, volunteered the lawyerlike explanation that the bank had anticipated no difficulties in the transaction because "Mercantile Bank was Dutch-owned at that time . . . it was hard to understand . . . that there would be the objection that was voiced with a change in ownership from one foreigner to another."

To equate Dutch and American ownership of a Canadian bank in 1963 was, of course, to be utterly innocent of the temper of Canadian nationalism, both historically and in respect to its growing preoccupation with the American presence. That this American unawareness may not have been wholly a private misapprehension is suggested by a Citibank memorandum reporting on the July 1963 meeting of Messrs. Rockefeller and MacFadden with Mr. Gordon, which concluded: "We had previously called on U.S. Ambassador Butterworth to inform him of our plans and he was most enthusiastic about our going into Canada."

Although the Mercantile Bank controversy resulted in barriers being erected against American penetration of the Canadian banking system, its larger, longer-run significance was threefold: (1) it spread and augmented Canadian nationalistic apprehensions from coast to coast; (2) it provided a kind of War of 1812 rallying point for the nationalists; as Professor Fayerweather put it, "in the later stages of the affair many Canadians had a sense of participation in a national struggle against the United States" [8]; and (3) even though Walter Gordon is not likely to rank with General Brock as a repulser of Yankee invaders, the affair went far to make him the principal spokesman against the threat, as perceived by the more militant nationalists, of American economic domination.

It is possible but not at all certain that if there had been no Mercantile Bank affair some other occasion would have produced the same results. While Walter Gordon and his followers were disappointed with the mildness of the Trudeau Government's 1972 proposals for screening foreign take-overs, there might well have been no such proposals (and their subsequent stiffening) if there had been no Gray Report in 1972, no Wahn Committee Report in the House of Commons in 1969, no Watkins Task Force Report on foreign ownership in 1968 (a major study launched in 1967 by the Pearson Government at Mr. Gordon's urging), no Mercantile Bank controversy from 1963 to 1967, no Gordon Royal Commission Report in 1957, and perhaps above all, no Walter Gordon with his nationalism as set forth under the titles: *Troubled Canada* (1961), and *A Choice for Canada: Independence or Colonial Status* (1966). The unfolding story of Canada's progressively more nationalistic stance on foreign investment during the past decade was not greatly overpersonalized in the title of the 1970 nationalistic tract: *Gordon to Watkins to You.* In restrospect, it is clear from the record, especially the public inquiries of this period, that Canada's nearly two decades of searching for a national policy on foreign investment were characterized by a spiraling inclination toward nationalistic restrictions. The Watkin Task Force Report of 1968 concluded with an avowal of the continuing, elemental concern for Canadian nationhood that has dominated this policy search: "The old National Policy served Canada in its day as an instrument of nation-building.... The challenges have changed and a new National Policy is required. The nation has been built, but its sovereignty must be protected and its independence maintained." [9]

Some students of this development distinguish between negative and positive nationalism. Professor Fayerweather, in his study of the Mercantile Bank case, while judging the specific legislative restrictions to have been an instance of "negative nationalism" concluded, perhaps prematurely in 1971 (prior to the 1973 Gray Report and the Foreign Investment Review Act of 1973):

... the greater strength still lies with the positive nationalists who are concerned about foreign investment but would counteract it by building up Canadian business without resort to actions which have a significant adverse effect on foreign companies.[10]

The record suggests that, overall, today's national policy is a complex, pragmatic mix of both negative and positive approaches. The underlying reality of both is a progressively aroused nationalism. Inevitably, large issues of political practicality as well as of economic wisdom have been involved in the search for acceptable foreign-investment policies. While the acceptability of restrictive policies now seems established, there is little indication that either negative or positive nationalism will exclusively dominate Canadian policies. The outlook is for more of both.

The complementarity of the two approaches is witnessed by the position of Walter Gordon himself who, even as he gained his reputation in Pearson's Cabinet as the foremost partisan of restrictive policies, was also one of the first proponents of the positive approach of creating a development corporation to promote and assist in the capital financing of greater domestic ownership for Canada's industries and resources. In late 1971, following eight years of what was regarded by many nationalists as "all deliberate delay," the Canadian Development Corporation (C.D.C.) was launched. It began with a 250 million dollar government investment and a potential equity capitalization of 2 billion dollars, the principal portion of which it was hoped would subsequently be subscribed by private investors. The C.D.C. as authorized by Parliament, is a hybrid creature born of public purpose, launched with government money but operated as a business expected to be a profitable investment enterprise. In little more than a year the C.D.C. took over or indicated an interest in acquiring several governmentally owned Crown corporations in petrochemicals and uranium production, as well as the government's 45 percent ownership interest in the mixed public-private consortium, Panarctic Oils, Ltd., an oil and gas exploration enterprise operating in the Arctic. The corporation also moved to become a participant in the Gas Arctic-Northwest Project, a consortium of Canadian and United States firms interested in building a gas pipeline into the Far North. It is too soon to

judge C.D.C.'s future as a business enterprise, but by 1975 its
assets had grown to nearly one billion dollars. It is already clear
that Ottawa looks to it as an affirmative agency for promotion
as well as protecting the national interest in economic
development. Whether through the C.D.C. or otherwise, it is
also clear that this national interest will press Canadian equity
control in such key enterprises as a northern pipeline for gas,
and the future exploitation of natural resources generally.
Indeed, aside from its merits as an investment, this presumably was the basic Canadian national interest behind the
C.D.C's dramatic move in 1973 to acquire effective ownership
control of the United States firm Texasgulf with its major
resource interests in Canada.

Some supporters of the C.D.C. profess to see it as a potential investment vehicle for new foreign capital willing to participate in a Canadian enterprise without exercising control.
The Texasgulf take-over by the C.D.C. has been viewed by
some as a first step in "buying Canada back" from American
control. More realistically, it may suggest that American
equity capital will be welcome if it is present as a noncon-
trolling interest. How much new minority equity capital
would be available from the outside on terms consonant with
the public purposes of the C.D.C. is an open question. The
answer will depend importantly on the C.D.C demonstrating
an orientation and managerial capability compatible with
profitable private investment. The future course of multinational corporations in the international community is also
involved. An international community hostile to foreign control of national industries but hospitable to outside minority
investment would likely stimulate opportunities for the
C.D.C as a partnership approach to Canada's industrial
development. There are already tangible indications of interest by the Japanese in such joint enterprises, particularly in the
natural resource industries of Alberta and British Columbia.
The eventual development of C.D.C. itself as a major vehicle
for minority foreign investment is still over the horizon, but it
has such a potential.

"Positive nationalism" is a capacious concept that occasionally has taken on epic proportions, encompassing nation-

building as well as countering the threat of American domination of such critical sectors as Canada's east-west lifelines of transportation and communication. In fact, there is no more spectacular instance of the continuing attraction-rejection theme in the United States-Canada relationship than the building of Canada's transcontinental railways. These undertakings were largely stimulated by the American presence, but ultimately realized and sustained by a determined Canadian nationalism. Much the same scenario was reenacted in creating the Canadian Broadcasting Corporation and Air Canada, both state-owned enterprises committed to building national cohesion. Such major instances of "positive nationalism" witness a significant fact of Canada's nationalism not widely appreciated by Americans, namely, that in matters deemed fundamental to the national interest, the precepts and interests of private enterprise are a far less formidable barrier to public ownership than is the case in the United States. Currently such projects as a Mackenzie Valley gas pipeline, the extension of an oil line to Montreal and the development of the Athabaska tar sands are being approached as efforts in which the public purpose must prevail. Indeed, not a few Canadians will be surprised if the semipublic C.D.C. does not ultimately go public in control as well as purpose.

At the same time neither Ottawa nor the provincial governments are indifferent to possibilities for furthering industrial development, trade, and greater Canadian control of industry and resources through assistance to private enterprises. Tax policies, governmental-promotion programs (including research and development grants), and a major national effort to achieve greater regional equalization are increasingly attuned to these objectives. In many instances these governmental-assistance programs either fall within accepted international practices or involve sufficiently special situations to be treated as exceptions. On the other hand, in both Canada and the United States, as indeed elsewhere, the boundary is becoming increasingly blurred between acceptable national-policy purposes and the internationally destructive practices of a progressively more protective economic nationalism using the "positive" approaches of taxation and subsidies. The danger is that these policy measures of modern government will be perverted into weapons of international economic warfare.

Positive nationalism in the form of assisting Canadian-owned enterprises, in contrast to policies aimed at restricting or eliminating foreign-controlled firms, it will be recalled, was the principle around which the Ontario Royal Commission on Book Publishing developed its major policy recommendations. Any other philosophy for restricting the reading fare available to Canadians would, in that Commission's view, risk unacceptable governmental interference with individual rights and the welfare of Canadian society. And yet, even this powerful consideration was ultimately qualified by a recommendation that foreign take-overs and new publishing ventures be subject to approval by an official screening agency, a sort of hedged bet against future confrontations between the right to read and the incalculable power of nationalism. The record shows that individual rights and preferences rarely prevail in such a showdown. In the related area of newspaper and magazine publishing, national-interest considerations were judged sufficient by the O'Leary Commission (1961) and by Parliament (1965) to justify the exclusion (with controversial exceptions for *Reader's Digest* and *Time*) of foreign-controlled publishers by denying income-tax deductibility to advertising in newspapers and periodicals with less than 75 percent Canadian ownership.

In other situations where the national interest in Canadian ownership and control has also been deemed paramount—the so-called key-sector enterprises—Canada has not hesitated to limit foreign-equity investment to a minority position and to prescribe requirements to assure or encourage domestic control or management. In certain key sectors such as public transport, federal ownership of major enterprises such as the Canadian National Railroad and Air Canada, along with public regulation of transportation as a mixed private-public industry, effectively limits the presence of large-scale foreign investment. In radio and TV broadcasting the same mix of public ownership and private enterprise exists. The Broadcasting Act of 1968 limits nonresident ownership in a private station to 20 percent, while making both the public-owned C.B.C. and the private broadcasters and cable companies subject to operating licenses and policies issued by the federal C.R.-T.C. In other key sectors the national interest in greater Canadian ownership and control is protected by such federal laws as the Canadian and British Insurance Companies Act as amended in 1957 and 1965, requiring a majority of directors to be resident Canadians and restricting share transfers to foreign ownership to 25 percent; the Loan Companies Act and the Trust Companies Act requiring not less than three fourths of the directors to be resident Canadians with limitations on transfer to foreign ownership similar to the insurance legislation. Similarly, mining, oil, and gas leases under federal control require at least 50-percent Canadian ownership; and as of 1970, foreign ownership in a uranium-mining property is limited to 33 percent. The list is by no means complete, but it gives a fair indication of the pragmatic thrust of Canadian policy in recent years as it has sought to be responsive on area-by-area, even a case-by-case basis (e.g., the Mercantile Bank and Denison Mines, Canada's largest uranium producer) to nationalistic concerns about a spreading American presence in Canadian business.

The fifteen years between the 1957 Royal Commission Report on Canada's Economic Prospects and the Foreign Takeovers Review Policy propounded by the Trudeau Government in 1972 was a period of spreading nationalistic concern which was reflected in a procession of investigations and a series of *ad hoc* actions. Two seemingly moderate governmental actions taken during this period can now be seen as important steps toward the development of a more systematic, comprehensive approach to the regulation of foreign investment. They were the passage of the Corporations and Labor Unions Returns Act of 1962, and the issuance in 1967 by the Minister of Trade and Commerce, the late Robert Winters, of "Some Guiding Principles of Good Corporate Behavior for Subsidiaries in Canada of Foreign Companies."

Although applicable to both domestic and foreign enterprises, in view of the dominance of the large American companies and the international United States-based labor unions on the Canadian scene, the Returns Act (CALURA) made it inevitable that in the future both American corporations and unions would be subject to increasingly sophisticated scrutiny. The development of adequate, meaningful statistics was an overdue, essential requisite for public understanding and policy formulation in this increasingly critical area of the Canada-United States relationship.

The 1967 "Principles of Good Corporate Behavior" were informal and voluntary, lacking the sanction of law. Coming when they did, however, and from a Minister with a highly respected background in Canadian business who was considered a possible successor to Lester Pearson, they served to bring the issue to the serious attention of corporate and governmental officials in a way that nationalist agitation had not been able to do up to that time. The style was non-provocative and the guiding principles took account of economic interests, but substantive nationalistic aims were not muted. They included development of export markets, greater processing in Canada of natural resources, utilization of Canadian sources of supply, research- and technological-development programs, retention of earnings for growth, Canadian personnel and outlook in management, a majority of Canadians as directors, opportunity for equity participation by Canadians, and support of national objectives.

The continuity of concern that has characterized the evolution of Canadian national policy on foreign investment is significantly evident both in the degree to which the "Canadian benefit" standards for acceptable foreign investment in the 1973 legislation were foreshadowed by the "Principles of Good Corporate Behavior" of 1967, and by the extent to which those principles were earlier reflected in the 1968 Watkins Task Force Report and the 1972 Gray Report, *Foreign Direct Investment In Canada,* as well as the more derivative Wahn report in 1969-70 on Canada-United States relations by the House of Commons Committee on External Affairs.

Americans familiar with a more impatient political process frequently fail to give sufficient attention to the fact that on a complicated federal-provincial issue such as the pros and cons of American investment, Canadian policy "grows" more than it is decided upon. Yet, by 1970, concern over foreign, especially American, ownership had reached a point where an active policy response by Ottawa was necessary. Accordingly, the Trudeau Government took what as a matter of practical politics had to be the final step before the government faced its moment of truth on the issue. A member of the Cabinet, the then Minister of Revenue, Herb Gray, was given "the responsibility of bringing forward proposals on foreign investment policy for the consideration of the government."

In early 1972, after nearly two years of the most comprehensive analysis the oft-studied subject may ever receive, and following a spate of sensational publicity caused by an incomplete leaked version, the five-hundred-page document, *Foreign Direct Investment In Canada*, popularly known as the "Gray Report," appeared. It was issued under "the authority of the Government of Canada," but without having either the status of official policy or the government's endorsement of "all aspects of its analysis." The Gray Report is incomparably required reading for Americans seeking a comprehensive view of the foreign-direct-investment question as it is perceived in Canada today.

The report's opening sentences set the stage:

> The degree of foreign ownership and control of economic activity is already substantially higher in Canada than in any other industrialized country and is continuing to increase.

> Nearly sixty percent of manufacturing in Canada is foreign controlled and in some manufacturing industries such as petroleum and rubber products foreign control exceeds ninety percent ... approximately eighty per cent of foreign control over Canadian manufacturing and natural resource industries rests in the United States.[11]

In addition to the statistical American presence portrayed, the report analyzed a broad spectrum of economic determinants—costs, benefits, and policy disadvantages of foreign investment in the Canadian situation as well as the potential impact of the multinational enterprise throughout the international community. Particular attention was focused on foreign take-overs of Canadian-owned companies. On the basis of incomplete data, and excluding take-overs financed by retained earnings of foreign-controlled firms already in Canada, take-overs jumped from nine in 1950 to 163 in 1970. The Report concludes that this has been "an important route through which foreign control of Canadian manufacturing activity has grown ... [while] the economic benefits of such takeovers are normally far fewer than those obtained through the starting up of new firms."

The Report prophetically suggested that "consideration might be given to the adoption of public policy establishing a degree of bias against foreign takeovers, especially of large Canadian firms, which places the onus on the prospective foreign purchaser to demonstrate the benefit of the proposed takeover to the Canadian economy." Out of this observation, and its important elaboration in Chapter 25 of the Report, came Canada's new national policy on foreign direct investment. Initially put forth in May 1972 as a bill to establish a Foreign Takeovers Review policy, it was replaced in January 1973 by a revised and extended Foreign Investment Review bill that passed Parliament in December 1973.

The Takeovers Policy Proposal of 1972 was criticized by militant nationalists and others, including Premier Davis of Ontario and labor leaders, as falling short of what was needed; the revised and expanded policy of the Foreign Investment Review Act of 1973, was also viewed by many, including some supporters, as essentially only a technical extension and clarification of the government's original policy position. The future may reveal, however, that in both the initial proposals and especially in their extension, longer steps were taken in the direction of more nationalistic policies than either the critics or the supporters of the new policy realized.

The government's revised and extended policy proposals reflected its traumatic setback in the fall election of 1972. The effort to picture the revised proposals as simultaneously strong and moderate was highlighted by Alastair Gillespie, successor to Jean-Luc Pepin as Minister of Industry, Trade and Commerce, when he described the new bill as "a substantial further step in the government's on-going response to the problems of foreign investment" while at the same time asserting that there was "no retroactivity or narrow nationalism reflected in this approach."

In fact, a comparison between the 1972 bill and the 1973 Act indicates clearly and significantly that the Trudeau Government concluded from the reaction to its initial proposal that the tide of Canadian nationalism was still incoming and required a substantially stronger policy response than merely screening take-overs. As presented to the House of Commons in May 1972, the earlier measure was limited to requiring "foreign companies seeking to buy out or take over an existing Canadian business above certain size [assets of 250,-000 dollars or gross revenues of three million dollars] . . . to demonstrate that the purchase will result in significant benefit," to Canada." In judging "significant benefit," five factors would be considered:

(a) level and nature of economic activity and employment
(b) participation by Canadians
(c) productivity, technological development, etc
(d) effect on competition
(e) compatibility with Canadian industrial and economic policies

Mr. Gray's initial presentation to the Commons repeated the judgment of the report that "take-overs are the form of foreign investment least likely to add significant benefits to the Canadian economy." Nevertheless, it was the potential benefit of take-overs to Canada "that persuaded the government that as a general policy a review process is preferable to other approaches such as designation of additional key sectors or mandatory Canadian shareholdings": the two other policy alternatives presented in the Gray Report. And with a prescience perhaps born of personal conviction acquired in the preparation of the Report, the Minister went on to say that "this decision, of course, does not rule out entirely the possibility that other approaches might be required at some time in the future"—a future closer at hand than he or his colleagues in the Government imagined.

In the event, the 1972 take-overs bill was not acted upon before Parliament rose for the fall election, and in January 1973 the Trudeau Government, now returned as a minority government dependent upon the militantly nationalistic National Democratic Party (N.D.P.) for a working majority and, indeed, its life, proposed a significantly stronger approach to the foreign-investment issue. The revised policy, presented under the rubric of "Foreign Investment Review" rather than "Foreign Takeovers," extended the scope of the take-over screening process to cover both new foreign direct investment and the expansion into "unrelated" business by foreign-controlled companies already established in Canada. As with the earlier proposal, the screening requirement applies only to enterprises having more than 250,000 dollars assets or annual revenue above three million dollars. The criteria for testing the "benefit to Canada" are essentially the same.

These extensions cannot help but extend significantly the policy reach and impact of the earlier proposal to put only take-overs from the outside to a proof of their benefit to Canada. Minister Gillespie sought to allay concern about the new policy by suggesting that confining the screening on the expansion of existing firms to "unrelated business" would avoid a "more interventionist policy of screening the expansion of existing foreign controlled firms in the line of business in which they were already operating," a policy which in addition to its "more interventionist" possibilities would, of certainty, have raised the troublesome issue of retroactivity.

Responding to inquiries as to why the government had expanded its screening policy, Minister Gillespie cited the view of certain provincial governments and "a significant majority" of Canadians who felt the initial policy had not gone far enough; by way of statistical support, he observed that "88 percent of the increase in foreign ownership in the Canadian economy occurred in the creation of new business or growth of existing firms, and that only 12 percent of the annual increase resulted from foreign takeovers." [12]

On the face of things it seems apparent that between May 1972 and January 1973, policy responded more to the political weather than to any change in the intrinsic nature of the problem. This in itself underscores one of the most important features of a national policy based on an *ad-hoc* screening of foreign investment, namely, its flexibility and selectivity. This flexibility could make the new policy highly vulnerable to emotional, short-range changes in the political climate as well as to the myriad interests of place and circumstance that bear down on any national policy based upon administrative judgment. Other nations with somewhat different foreign-investment problems now use screening processes, particularly to pass upon major new foreign direct investment; only experience will tell whether such a national policy will work satisfactorily under Canada's "decentralized federalism" with probably upward of two hundred take-overs screened annually. When the second phase of the Act—covering new investments and "unrelated" expansion—becomes effective, an additional three to four hundred cases may be screened yearly.

The broader screening called for in the second part of the new policy was originally planned to take effect in 1975 following a year's experience screeening take-overs. Early in 1975, however, pressure on the Trudeau Government by the provinces resulted in an unspecified postponement. Bespeaking the critical disappointment of most nationalists, the *Toronto Star* observed that "Industry Minister Alastair Gillespie is thumbing his nose at Parliament by allowing his provincial counterparts to talk him out of proclaiming the second part of the Foreign Investment Review Act immediately. . . . what makes Gillespie think the provinces will be better disposed toward the legislation after further contemplation?" [13]

This unanswered question reaffirms the early evident fact that whatever else is uncertain about the new national policy, it is certain to add a major area of potential conflict to the already heavily burdened relationship of the Federal government with Canada's ten regionally diverse provincial governments. Indeed, one of the less newsworthy but nonetheless important changes introduced into the revised bill was an explicit recognition of the interest of the provinces; the fifth and final criterion for determining benefit to Canada now goes beyond the initial "compatibility . . . with Canadian industrial and economic policies" by adding "taking into consideration industrial and economic policy objectives enunciated by the government or legislature of any province likely to be significantly affected by the acquisition or establishment." The possibility for trouble is underscored by the presumably reliable report that prior to the enactment of the bill, the Premier of New Brunswick sought unsuccessfully to have his province exempted from it. Future pressures for ad hoc exemptions will inevitably be formidable and could seriously compromise screening as a national policy.

Over and above all other perplexities and uncertainties is the Canadian fact that constitutionally as well as politically the regulation of foreign ownership and control is not a matter solely within the control of the federal government. Ten provincial governments are also very much involved.

The four Atlantic provinces (New Brunswick, Newfoundland, Nova Scotia, and Prince Edward Island) can be expected to adhere formally to federal policy norms. Substantively, however, the overriding self-interest of the region in greater economic development and more employment will put great pressure on any national screening process to accommodate promising foreign investment projects. The history of Canada is replete with national policies that have gone aground on the shoals of provincial objections.

Quebec, of course, is a very special situation. Here nationalism is the French-Canadian variety, which bears little resemblance to Ontario's nationalism when it concerns the American investment presence. As matters stand today, Quebec's provincial autonomy is and will continue to be the dominant reality to be reckoned with. Foreign direct investment will be scrutinized on an *ad hoc* basis by both Ottawa and the province and, as indicated earlier, the Quebec interest will be sharply asserted in such key sectors as book publishing and financial enterprises, including insurance and investment. If foreign investment fits Quebec's sense of her needs, particularly in respect to more employment and industrial development, including adherence to French as "the language of work," it will not be discouraged. American capital will be welcomed at least as much as English-Canadian investment, and except in rare situations where Ottawa cannot avoid a confrontation, e.g., a "key sector" case, Quebec's provincial interest and policy will likely determine "the significant benefit to Canada."

Assuming that separatist agitation is no longer a major deterrent to outside capital (which, if unemployment can be contained, is a reasonable assumption), the outlook for foreign investment in Quebec is positive. This was stated very bluntly by Quebec's minister of Resources, Gilles Masse, at the opening of a 75-million-dollar plant at the Canadian Johns-Manville Jeffrey mine: "No matter what anyone might say to the contrary . . . Quebec just can't do it alone right now. We need foreign investment but that foreign investment will have to think Québécois before the government approves anything." [14]

Not surprisingly, Ontario, the historic heartland of both English-Canadian nationalism and the American presence, has recently been most conspicuous among the provinces as a proponent of more nationalistic policies. Premier William Davis's Progressive-Conservative government has featured its recent initiative in requiring a majority of resident Canadian directors on the boards of corporations chartered by Ontario. Correspondingly, Premier Davis noted critically Ottawa's failure to include such a requirement in its May 1972 screening proposals. In January 1973, the Trudeau Government announced, along with its newly strengthened Foreign Investment Review policy, that the Canada Corporations Act would shortly be amended to include such a requirement for federally incorporated companies. The requirement itself is not likely to restrict foreign direct investment, but the political background of its adoption confirms other indications that nationalistic policies, at least those involving small economic cost, are increasingly attractive to all three of Canada's principal parties.

Ontario, it should be noted, preceded Ottawa's "Gray Report" with its own study of foreign investment, an investigation carried out by an interdepartmental Task Force under

C. P. Honey, which in December 1971 recommended "moderate Canadian nationalism as the basic framework for policy formulation." The "Honey Report" reflected much the same concern as various federal studies mentioned earlier, namely: "a continued 'open door' policy involves incipient threats to this country's continued economic independence and its cultural distinctiveness." It will be recalled that Ontario also led the way in initiating a comprehensive investigation of the foreign ownership issue in book publishing and distribution which, along with the "Honey Report," came out in favor of a review process to screen foreign investment.

Ontario has also discovered, however, that even "moderate nationalism" invites problems of private protectionism and interprovincial competition. For example, Ontario's study of the investment industry (Moore Report, 1970) concluded that "any further non-resident control over Canadian securities firms ... should be prohibited," but a Quebec committee (Bouchard Report, 1971) studied the matter and recommended "that, within acceptable limits, foreign securities firms from various parts of the world be welcomed to Quebec so that Quebec may have the easiest possible access to various foreign sources of capital in order that the dependence of Quebec on specific groups of non-Quebec firms be diminished." The Quebec committee rejected the Ontario suggestion of seeking to treat the securities industry as a key sector of the Canadian economy in order to restrict competition from American firms; to the contrary, it believed that "Canadian securities firms might operate more efficiently if they had to compete with a greater number of American firms."

The Ontario legislature's Committee on Economic and Cultural Nationalism, which took up in 1972 where the Interdepartmental Task Force left off, recently heard two suggestions that indicate how strong the affinity is between an aroused nationalism and self-interested "protectionism": (1) the Association of Canadian Television and Radio Artists proposed that CBC television be limited to 15-percent foreign content, and that by 1980 the private stations be reduced to 30-percent non-Canadian content; (2) Senator Keith Davey (chairman, Canada's Special Senate Committee on Mass

Media) urged that all advertising agencies be required to be 80-percent Canadian-owned, and that all advertising used in Canada should be exclusively Canadian-produced.[15]

In the three prairie provinces (Manitoba, Saskatchewan, and Alberta), Canada's search for a sense of national identity has had to compete with an historic sense of separateness —economically, culturally and politically—as between the West and everything east of Winnipeg. Modern transportation and communication have moderated this sense of regional alienation, but it still remains a powerful reality. In 1972, Trudeau's liberal party, without a premier in any of the four western provinces, was unable to win even a respectable handful of western seats in Parliament, and despite its dramatic victory as a majority government in 1974 it failed to elect a single member from Alberta. The growing tendency continues in the prairie provinces and British Columbia toward what might be termed provincial-nationalism or at least nationalism on provincial terms.

Up to 1973 nationalism in the West, except for the issue of land ownership, was mainly a spreading sentiment rather than substantive policies. But increasingly, it is becoming manifest in public actions as well as private attitudes. For example, bitter nationalistic objection prevented the city of Calgary from employing an American chief of police even though, and undoubtedly in part because, Alberta, with its large American presence in the oil and gas industry, is sometimes derisively referred to as the Texas of the North. In fact, Alberta, under Premier Lougheed's Progressive-Conservative government, has been the leader in the western provinces in developing a stance of provincial nationalism. It has demanded more favorable treatment from Ottawa on pricing and taxation policies for oil and gas, and on industrial development as well as such traditional western grievances as tariffs, freight rates, and agricultural marketing. Alberta's dominant position in proven oil and gas resources, plus the projected development of the famed Athabaska tar sands, puts the province close to the heart of Canada's search for an energy policy. The 1973 international oil crisis and especially Ottawa's taxation responses exploded a federal-provincial conflict with Alberta that threatened to rival Ottawa's Quebec problems. It is a certain thing that for at least the next decade there will be a singular "Alberta fact" in both Canadian energy policies and, perforce, in Canada's relations with the United States.

Further west, the energy needs of the United States in other forms are creating fresh stresses. Public-opinion polls in British Columbia show the "new nationalism" making inroads in the "good feeling" that has long characterized American-Canadian relations in that region; the deterioration is increasingly evident in public attitudes toward such important policies as the shared development of hydropower, e.g, raising water levels in Canada with higher United States dams, and in British Columbia's fear of oil spills from United States tankers carrying Alaskan oil now that the trans-Alaskan pipeline is going forward. In turn, the 1973-74 decision of British Columbia to disregard contractual commitments for the supply of natural gas to the United States, leaving American users to bear the whole burden of a short-fall in supply, spread dismay and distrust in both industrial and official circles in the United States.

A more overt American nationalism is beginning to show in the west as well as elsewhere in border communities. In Whatcom County, Washington, a "Canadian land rush" is charterized in a leading American liberal magazine as a "reverse invasion" from Vancouver, British Columbia (Canada's fastest growing province) and the local director of parks foresees" the pressure for county park facilities by Canadians is going to reach the point of political decision: should we keep the Canadians out? The feeling of many people I talk to is one of open animosity." The spread of such feelings is at best an early warning affirmation of the well worn but uncomfortable truth that nationalistic exclusion is inevitably a reciprocating process.[16]

In 1975, Canada moves from nearly twenty years of searching for a national policy on foreign investment to the task of making a screening policy work, both nationally and regionally, both economically and politically.

On July 10, 1975, Canada's search for a new National Policy was once again sharply focused on international trade policy

by the issuance of "a consensus document," the product of a
three-year study by the prestigious Economic Council of
Canada, recommending "that parallel with its participation in
the current multilateral trade negotiations, the Canadian
government actively explore . . . an open-ended free trade
area with . . . the United States, the EEC, and Japan. . . ." The
Council's report, with its head-on advocacy of a free trade
policy (excluding crude oil and natural gas "at least initially"),
may or may not stir the national discussion it invites but it
was forthwith denounced by the nationalistically oriented
Toronto Star for not "dealing with foreign ownership rather
than advocating a further sell-out to the south." To the contrary, the Council's concluding judgment is that its proposed
policy is most likely to produce economic wellbeing "in a
country that remains politically autonomous and internally
united" [17]—the two prime, abiding concerns of Canadian national policy and statecraft. Whatever its impact in the north,
the Council's report is required reading south of the border.

*   *   *   *   *   *   *

The Americanization syndrome will continue to cause anxiety among Canadians. No single policy, even on foreign investment, can work a cure. The problem is too deeply rooted
in geography and history and too omnipresent in Canadian
life for it to be otherwise. The American presence, in trade and
investment, is inescapably intertwined with any search for a
national industrial strategy. Economic interests will continue
in confrontation with various manifestations of economic nationalism; the direction of national policy will probably fluc-
tuate depending on internal economic conditions and sometimes on international events as well. If, as recent reports
suggest, Canada is becoming somewhat less attractive to new
foreign investment, a screening policy may be nationalistically
of secondary importance compared to tax policies designed to
promote more Canadian ownership and more domestic
processing of raw materials.

Few policy predictions are possible, for an overall judgment may be ventured. Whether viewed nationally or regionally, Canadian nationalism has moved haltingly but unmistakably from precept to public policy. The outlook for some years is for more of the same in both cultural and economic affairs.

Notes

1. In *Close the 49th Parallel, Etc.: supra*, pp. 26, 32.
2. *Independence the Canadian Challenge*, Rotstein and Lax, Editors (Toronto, 1972), pp. 76-77.
3. *Foreign Direct Investment in Canada* (Ottawa: Government of Canada, 1972), p. 521, and Mitchell Sharp, *International Perspectives* (Autumn 1972), p. 4.
4. *Globe and Mail*, April 16, 1973.
5. 64 *Queen's Quarterly*, August 1957, pp. 305, 320.
6. *Final Report*, Royal Commission on Canada's Economic Prospects (Ottawa, 1958), p. 390.
7. John Fayerweather, "The Mercantile Bank Affair," *Columbia Journal of World Business*, Vol. VI, No. 6 (Nov.-Dec. 1971), p. 41.
8. Fayerweather, "Bank Affair," p. 47.
9. *Foreign Ownership and the Structure of Canadian Industry*, Report of the Task Force on the Structure of Canadian Industry, January 1968.
10. Fayerweather, "Bank Affair," pp. 41, 50.
11. Gray Report, p. 5.
12. *International Canada*, January 1973, p. 19; *The Globe and Mail, The Ottawa Citizen*, January 25, 1973.
13. The *Toronto Star*, March 13, 1975, p. C4.
14. *The Montreal Star*, July 13, 1973.
15. *International Canada* (January 1973), p. 19.
16. "The Canadians Are Coming," Mary Alice Kellogg, *The Nation*, June 14, 1975.
17. *Looking Outward—A New Trade Strategy for Canada*, report of the Economic Council of Canada (Ottawa: Information Canada, 1975).

PART III

The United States National Interest and the Relationship

CHAPTER 8

An Independent Canada: A "Fundamental Tenet"

December 7, 1971 is not likely to offer serious competition with an earlier December 7 for top billing in American history, but as things go in the United States-Canada relationship, it may prove to have been a notable occasion. The Prime Minister of Canada gave the Parliament a potentially historic report of a discussion he had in Washington the previous day with the President of the United States. The meeting of the two leaders was of special interest, at least in Canadian eyes: several months earlier, within a thirty-day period, the American President had twice made unhappy news from coast to coast in Canada.

On August 15, President Nixon's dramatically announced new economic policy, with its imposition of a surcharge on United States imports, had produced an instant trauma throughout Canada. There were emotions of anger and short-lived disbelief—the United States evidently did not understand Canada's special position in the matter—and left United States-Canada economic relations, so far as Canadians were concerned, in a limbo of high anxiety. On September 16, Canadian sensibilities received a second seismic jolt. President

Nixon, in an effort to reassure the American public about trade discussions with Japan, announced at a White House news conference: "After the Japanese were here I found that, both from the information they gave me and the information we had ourselves, that Japan is our biggest customer in the world." Coming as it did hard on the August 15 shock, the President's confusion of Japan with Canada as the best customer of the United States seemed to many Canadians to confirm their worst fears as to where Canada stood in the hierarchy of American interests and understanding.

Naturally enough, these American happenings created problems for Prime Minister Trudeau, whose political leadership was under attack on two fronts. On the one hand, he faced the growing militancy of Canadian nationalism with its insistence that the country's independence was being (or had been) sold out to the Americans; on the other hand, he was charged, however paradoxically, with having brought the surcharge and other forms of United States wrath down on Canada's head because he had permitted the United States special relationship to languish.

The Prime Minister's visit to the White House was made on his own initiative to counter these two contradictory thrusts of Canadian concern. The President, having been well briefed this time, was anxious to do what he could to repair things and be reassuring. He succeeded to the point where the Prime Minister forthwith publicly pronounced the President's reassurances as "fantastic," a characterization that some in Canada found a little fulsome. Most of those Americans who noticed the press reports at all were simply puzzled that something they took for granted should be "fantastically" significant to the Canadian Prime Minister.

Immediately on returning to Canada, Mr. Trudeau formally reported the presidential statements to Parliament:

> One of the purposes of my visit was to seek reassurance from the President, and it can only come from him, that it is neither the intention nor the desire of the United States that the economy of Canada become so dependent upon the United States in terms of a deficit trading

pattern that Canadians will inevitably lose independence of economic decisions. . . . He assured me that it was in the clear interests of the United States to have a Canadian neighbour, not only independent both politically and economically but also one which was confident that the decisions and policies in each of these sectors would be taken by Canadians in their own interests, in defence of their own values, and in pursuit of their own goals. . . . We are a distinct country, we are a distinct people, and our remaining such is, I was assured, in the interests of the United States and is a fundamental tenet of the foreign policies of that country as expressed by the Nixon administration.

The White House itself issued no statement about the reassurances, but neither has the Prime Minister's version ever been questioned. Indeed, the meeting of the two leaders was barely news in the United States. The matter obviously had far greater importance for Canada; the difference epitomizes the problem of imbalance in the affairs of the two countries. However taken for granted such reassurances may seem to Americans, and however gratuitously they grate on the sensibilities of those nationalists who understandably do not enjoy having the United States seem to "bestow" independence on Canada, the fact is that the President's words were addressed to the most abiding issue in the relationship. The occasion contributes significantly to American understanding in two respects: first, the character of the reassurances the Prime Minister sought highlights the relevance of the independence issue between Canada and the United States; secondly, the Prime Minister's shrewd perception and handling of the matter made it clear that contrary to conventional wisdom, the United States does in fact have a contribution to make in helping to obviate the gathering danger to both countries of a runaway anti-American Canadian nationalism.

The validity of the cliché that Americans take Canada for granted is borne out by the unexamined ease with which in little more than one hundred years we have switched from an assumption that Canada's manifest destiny was annexation by the United States to today's benign awareness that Canada has anything to worry about from us. It is only one example of American ignorance about things Canadian, but it is a fact that until very recently it had not occurred to more than a handful of scholars and diplomatists that a well-intentioned United States, with its spreading American presence in Canadian life, might be regarded as (let alone actually be) a threat to a viable Canadian nationhood.

Greater awareness of this Canadian concern could be immensely instructive to American understanding. It brings to the surface two ill-founded premises which underlie American assumptions about the United States-Canadian relationship, namely, our intentions being good, no harm can result, and since the two countries are so similar, what is true for the United States is also true for Canada.

Americans do take their genuine good intentions toward Canada for granted. This has dulled our sensitivity to the increasingly critical perception by many Canadians of the consequences of American influences in their national life. Perhaps even more deleterious is the American tendency to assume that, because there are many similarities and shared experiences, the two nations are alike in all fundamental things. There is probably no firmer tenet of Canadian faith than that this is not so. Few things offer better proof than the fundamentally different posture of the two countries in respect to national independence. For nearly two hundred years Americans have been able to take independent nationhood for granted. It therefore comes naturally to assume that Canada also takes her independence for granted. The hard fact is, however, that she never has, she does not now, and for the foreseeable future will not be able to take independent nationhood for granted in any sense similar to the United States. Well into the twentieth century, the British tie precluded it. Today, a spreading American presence keeps the issue of independence a live concern.

Nations, of course, have long been familiar with the practice of promoting and protecting another nation's independence as a way of serving their own national interest. The Monroe Doctrine is a classical instance. Actually, the long history of the United States fostering the national independence of others began with Canada. Indeed, American efforts to promote Canada's independence predated the United States as a nation. Washington, Franklin, Lafayette, and other notables of the American Revolution at various times sought unsuccessfully, through both persuasion and force, to further the rebellion against the British Crown by getting the Canadians to join their cause.

The decisive failure of the American effort to "liberate" Canada from British rule by military force came in the War of 1812. One can only speculate on what form the issue of Canadian independence would have taken if these early American incursions had succeeded, but it is probably safe to say that the issue of an independent Canada would not have disappeared; almost certainly it would have resurfaced as an earlier, militant call for a *Québec Libre*.

The American national interest in the independence of Western Hemisphere nations as expressed in the Monroe Doctrine was more implicit than explicit with respect to Canada prior to the rise of the Axis Powers. President Franklin Roosevelt gave it explicit avowal in 1938 at Kingston, Ontario, declaring: "I give you assurance that the people of the United States will not stand idly by if domination of Canadian soil is threatened by any other Empire." Following Roosevelt's earlier statement in 1936, that the United States was prepared to defend its neighbor against aggression, the Kingston assurance and the Ogdensburg Joint Defense Agreement of 1940 made it unmistakably clear that the United States was in fact prepared to protect the independence of Canada against others. From World War II on through the Cold War and the advent of intercontinental bombers and missiles, this was readily translated into a concern for the protection of Canada as necessary to America's military defense.

This kind of concern for another country's independence has, of course, long been familiar to powerful states in the pursuit of their political and security interests. But if President Nixon had not gone beyond this in his December 1971 reassurances to Mr. Trudeau, he would not have been responsive to Canada's deepest concern—the integrity of her nationhood. The truly significant policy propounded by the American President was that Canada's need to be *independent of the United States*, politically, economically, and culturally, is similarly in the national interest of the United States.

The contemporary American presence and Canadian concern about it being what they are, such an avowal of the American position cannot escape being judged as a portent of things to come. Certainly it was no mere reiteration of juridical rights, and, if it was not meant to be taken seriously in Canada, it would be irresponsible for an American President to assure a Canadian Prime Minister that it is "in the clear interests of the United States to have a Canadian neighbour, not only independent both politically and economically but also one which was confident that the decisions and policies in each of these sectors would be taken by Canadians in their own interests in defence of their own values, and in pursuit of their own goals." No previous presidential utterance ever proclaimed the American interest in a truly independent Canada so clearly.

All of which is to the good, provided, but only provided, American officialdom and Americans generally understand and remain committed to such Canadian independence as a "fundamental tenet" of American policies, attitude, and interest. The grievous damage to the relationship that would follow any fundamental divergence from this commitment can hardly be other than painfully clear; the Nixon-Trudeau meeting put the matter beyond finessing.

Parenthetically, although the primary burden of giving reality to this "fundamental tenet" is on Americans and United States policy, Canada in her own interest has a role of restraint and wisdom to play that inescapably will have more than a small bearing on the long-run viability of Canadian independence as a United States national interest.

Such a national interest is not familiar to the American public. The concept itself has had so little analytical attention that most practitioners and students of the relationship would have trouble spelling out what "clear interests of the United States" the president had in mind. Without the support of such analysis and understanding even presidential assurances are likely to be wasting assets. The need is to support sentiment with specifics as to the United States interest in this kind of Canadian independence.

The matter can be approached negatively by picturing the likely consequences from a progressively less independent Canada. First and inescapably, the very existence of Canada as a nation would be at issue. It is no less true today that historically that Canada's national cohesion is grounded in its ability and will to be independent of the United States. It is highly unlikely that Canada, as a client-state of the United States, would hold together as a nation. Quebec separatism and other internal strains are apparently less threatening today, but the past decade has shown that Canada's margin of national cohesion is narrower than many Canadians and most Americans had assumed. For the foreseeable future, American policy as well as Canadian leadership must reckon with the revealed reality that Canada, as a nation, could break. The complications for the United States in such an outcome are beyond calculation. And well before the final unraveling of Canada, every United States national interest in the relationship would have been corroded by the hostility that dependence breeds. Of all such negative consequences, the most likely would be the progressive impairment of any possibility that the United States-Canada relationship may in due course evolve into an optimum interdependence of two distinct societies.

Viewed positively and functionally, the United States stake in an independent Canada is grounded not in Canada but in the United States. It is in the self-interest of a great power to be exposed to knowledgeable scrutiny from the outside which is free of both the hostility of an adversary and the acquiescence of a sycophant. An independent Canada alone meets this need.

One of the tenets of American society is that its pluralism, its constitutional freedoms, and its democratic processes assure the nation of a measure of self-criticism sufficient to protect its policies from unexposed error. The historical record generally supports the proposition that the nation's errors have rarely flourished for long simply for want of exposure, but the time lag between "a voice crying in the wilderness" and the straightening of the path has sometimes been rather long.

The nation's experience with the Vietnam war testified convincingly that American self-criticism is far from being a paper tiger, but equally important the experience demonstrated the high degree of interaction in a communication-intensive world between a nation's self-criticism and that coming from outside. American critics of the war might have prevailed on their own, but criticism from the outside constantly played a confirming, fortifying role and was a sufficient factor to worry American officialdom. Although Canadian public criticism of the war was slow to gather and remained mostly moderate, it was taken seriously by Americans. On the one occasion when Lester Pearson, the Canadian Prime Minister, ventured to expose his views to the American public on the desirability of a pause in the bombing, President Johnson was—to use a Texas-sized understatement—not amused.

Criticism of the United States by Canadians in the course of any given year will touch most subjects in the spectrum of public policy and private life. In form it ranges from starchy diplomatic notes, academic tomes, editorials, the maledictions of such groups as the N.D.P. and the Committee for an Independent Canada to the bantering *veritas in vino* of business conventions and hunting lodges. Whether official or private, criticism is not easier to accept because it comes from a neighbor or friend. Canadian criticism on occasion can be captious, even moralistic (Secretary of State Acheson felt that Ottawa preferred to raise mundane matters "to the plane of high principle"), but it is rarely vindictive. Except for the hypernationalists, the criticism is usually more regretful than aggressively bitter and it seems to have a built-in inevitability about it that makes it almost an expected part of the relationship. Informed as it is by propinquity and today's ubiquitous American presence, Canadian criticism is intimately knowledgeable, sometimes uncomfortably so.

Canada's China policy is one of the clearest examples of the value to the United States of an independent Canada, and also of the degree to which fear of United States resentment of policy divergence can stifle Canadian independence. As early as 1950, under the leadership of Prime Minister St. Laurent and Lester Pearson, then Minister of External Affairs, Canada was disposed to follow the lead of Britain and India in extending recognition to Peking. She held off, however, and the decision itself was delayed for another twenty years, largely because, as St. Laurent's biographer, Dale Thomson, states, "The possible advantages were outweighted by the disadvantages within Canada and in relations with her neighbor." Domestic political difficulties were real, but in weighing them Mr. Pearson never made a secret of his judgment that the matter had not seemed worth "a first-rate row with Washington." Yet the Canadian government's divergence of view was no secret to Washington. Over the years, the possibility of eventual recognition was freely discussed in the Canadian press and public circles, as well as the academic community, all very much in contrast to the situation in the United States where serious discussion of the subject was immobilized in a bipartisan freeze that loosened a little in the early 1960s, but hardened again as the American situation in Vietnam worsened.

We do not as yet have the full story behind either the Canadian recognition of Peking in 1970, or the ensuing Ping-Pong charade which preceded the United States-Chinese rapprochement in 1971. But unless there are later revelations that totally discredit what is now known, it seems certain that the Canadian initiative was one of the significantly "favorable circumstances" that helped both the American public and United States officialdom to break out of the dangerous, mutually reinforcing immobility that for twenty years characterized the United States-Chinese standoff. In this matter as in few others, the osmosis of influence was from north to south.

China policy also provides a classic example of the degree to which the United States national interest in an independent Canada can be compromised by a Canada which lacks confidence in its own capacity to pursue a divergent course. As the diplomats are fond of saying, there is fear of inducing a "counterproductive" United States reaction. The attitudes of the American Congress and press are particularly important. Canada gives special weight to congressional sentiment as the best single indicator of both the direction and intensity of American national feelings. John W. Holmes, a former assistant undersecretary in the Department of External Affairs and an astute student of the United States relationship, said of the early decision not to recognize Peking: "Direct pressure from Washington was not so much a factor as Canadian uneasiness about provoking the wrath of the U.S. Congress."

Canadian diffidence may well have adversely affected us in this matter. We can only speculate as to whether recognition of China in the 1950s by Canada and others, perhaps including the United States, might have contributed to a vastly different Vietnam history in the 1960s.

Although American observers have given Canada considerable credit for leading the way on the recognition of China, Canadians generally have understandably refrained from claiming to have led the United States out of the wilderness. In a December 1971 interview with James Reston, not published textually in *The New York Times*, Prime Minister Trudeau, while disclaiming such a role for Canada, did spell out his belief in the value of Canadian initiatives:

> . . . because we're a smaller and more manageable society . . . I think we can afford to take some risks of opening up new avenues which we think are correct. For even if they are incorrect we will be slapped down by events or force of circumstances or by our friends without great adverse consequences on peace and stability in the world. But for a power like yourselves, if you are naïve and your confidence doesn't breed confidence, but rather brings a terrible response from other countries, then it is of much greater moment not only for you but for the whole world, than if we make a mistake.

Whether or not the servant girl's justification of her indiscretion—"but ma'm, it's such a little baby"—has as much to be said for it in international affairs as Prime Minister Trudeau suggests, there can be little doubt that divergent Canadian initiatives on occasion can provide the United States with a sort of vicarious experience against which to make a more confident judgment of its alternatives.

Parenthetically, but not unimportantly, it should be noted that the United States stake in the success or failure of Canadian-policy divergences may be fully as great in domestic affairs as in foreign policy. A notable instance is found in a 1971 study of the United States Advisory Commission on Intergovernmental Relations entitled "In Search of Balance: Canada's intergovernmental Experience." This report, as described by the Commission Chairman, Robert E. Merriam, "focuses its attention on a comparative analysis of Canadian experience relating to selected intergovernmental fiscal tensions prevalent in the United States.... The Commission's concern centers on an analysis and description of Federal-Provincial relations, financing of public education and social welfare, and Provincial-local relations."

As the United States moves toward radically new fiscal relationships between the federal government and the states, and of both to local communities, the more venturesome and varied Canadian experience with these relationships, particularly with revenue sharing, may be especially useful. A Canadian political scientist, Pauline Jewett, with firsthand experience as a member of Parliament, has described Canada as a United States "window" for observing social experiments, and "as a kind of loyal opposition to traditional conservatism in the United States." Canadians take a special pride in their particular brand of government as a combination of some of the better features of both the British and the American systems. A growing interest on the part of Americans in the social policies of an independent Canada could serve significant United States domestic interests and at the same time strengthen the relationship.

Understandably, Canada's role as critic and occasional frontfunner of untried policies is not an attribute that lends itself to being featured by either country. But there is an international function of Canadian independence of great potential importance to all nations, perhaps especially to the United States, that does thrive on being widely acknowledged.

It is Canada's capacity for being accepted as a sufficiently disinterested member of the international community to be entrusted with responsibilities for which others, by reason of power or other circumstances, are not eligible.

For a considerable time after World War II, especially during the deepest freeze of the Cold War, there was a widely held view in the international community that Canada was peculiarly well suited to play what has been called a "mediatory role in world affairs." "Middle powermanship," with its accommodating, imprecise view of what middle meant, became in the eyes of many Canadians a way of being idealistically on the "side of the angels" while still remaining in geopolitical realities allied with the United States. And as things then stood most other nations, including the United States, welcomed the existence of such a Canada. However the Canadian middle-power role was perceived, it assumed a Canada that, while fundamentally friendly to the point of alliance with the United States, could still be regarded by the Communist countries and especially the third world as sufficiently independent not to be classed as a spear bearer for "American imperialism."

This benign ambivalence was put to good use by a generation of remarkable diplomatists, led by Lester Pearson, in rendering distinctive service to the international community. It was employed in such major undertakings as the resolution of the Suez crisis in 1956, the United Nations Emergency Force in the Middle East, the United Nations operations in the Congo, United Nations peacekeeping in Cyprus, as well as the work of the largely frustrated tripartite Commission for Supervision and Control in Indochina. From 1945 through 1970, Canada actually participated in ten United Nations peacekeeping operations.

In 1968, with the advent of the Trudeau Government, Canada undertook a comprehensive reappraisal of which national interests and principles should guide her foreign policies in a changing world. As the 1970 White Paper, "Foreign Policy for Canadians," put it: "International institutions which had been the focus and instrument of much of Canada's policy were troubled" and "the world powers could no longer

be grouped in clearly identifiable ideological camps." A combination of considerations—some internal, such as the
mounting crisis in French Canada, and others external—led
the Trudeau Government explicitly, if perhaps gratuitously,
to reject the typecasting of Canada "as the 'helpful fixer' in
international affairs."

Yet despite Canada's 1973 decision to terminate its unsatisfactory experience as a supervisor of the Vietnam truce, and
accepting the prospect that Canada's middle-power heyday is
a thing of the past, there remains a need for such a nation to
serve what might be fairly designated the disinterested interests of peace. A Canada that has practiced, as the 1970 White
Paper adjures, an unrelenting cultivation of her national interest in remaining "secure as an independent political entity," can hardly fail to be a source of strength in the international community. As was once again demonstrated in the
1973 Israeli-Arab cease-fire and in Cyprus in 1974-75, Canada's
independence must rate high as a national interest of both the
United States and the rest of the world as well.

While most policy problems in the relationship can be met
within a relatively short time-frame, having Canada regarded
as genuinely independent of the United States requires sustained United States sensitivity which must be developed
through a variety of situations over a period of time. Without
it, public statements of either presidents or prime ministers at
a moment of need will not be convincing. Incidentally, this
aspect of the American interest is very different from the fairly
common Canadian view that United States gets kudos from
other nations for behaving well towards Canada. There is little
evidence that such is the case; it is largely a pleasant Canadian
view of the way it ought to be.

Finally and most fundamentally, all other United States
national interests in Canada—economic, political, defense,
and cultural—depend upon the relationship's psychological
health. A confident, independent Canada may not be the
dominant, certainly it is not the only United States interest,
but it assuredly is the keystone of all other United States
national interests in the Canada-U.S. relationship.

A decade ago Canada's perceptive scholar-statesman,

Douglas Le Pan, identified this interest as a potential fashioning force in a healthy relationship: "If all the United States' dealings with Canada could be coloured with some continuing concern for Canadian independence, then arguments that now often seem at cross purposes would begin to fall into place... At no point am I suggesting that particular American interests should be disregarded... concern for the independence, for the independent strength [of Canada] ... should be regarded as forming part of the national interest of the United States and ... it should not be overlooked in the course of particular negotiations or of general planning."[1]

As things stand today, the *sine qua non* of the relationship's well-being is that Canadian independence should pass current with Canadians themselves. It was, therefore, no idle thing that Mr. Trudeau chose to feature the President's commitment to "a Canadian neighbour ... which was confident" of its independence of choice and decision. Actually, such Canadian confidence is still, and for the foreseeable future is likely to remain, an uncertain thing that generates a kind of highly self-conscious nationalism. The concern Americans share with most Canadians is to prevent an essentially positive nationalism from deteriorating into a frustrated, debilitating, neurotic preoccupation with the United States as the cause of all that's wrong and uncertain in Canada.

The reality of this danger is increasingly recognized in Canada. The respected Canadian academician, A. E. Safarian, has referred to many Canadians as being in a state akin to "self-induced paranoia"[2] and a well-known journalist, Raoul Engel of the *Financial Post* of Toronto, in reporting on a newly established Canadian-American conference center, mentioned certain critical Canadian reactions to it as "a response that suggested how deeply suspicious—almost paranoid—some of us have become over any kind of collaborative venture with the United States."[3]

Somewhat paradoxically, Canadian nationalism has become more militant at the very time that Canada's foreign policy has taken a more independent stance than perhaps ever before. Indeed, this seeming paradox and the inability of the doomsayers to deal with it convincingly have been something of a handicap to the cause of the more extreme nationalists. But at bottom, both Canada's heated-up nationalism and her more independent foreign policy are reactions to the same thing—a spreading American presence and a growing fear of undue dependence on the United States relationship.

Notes

1. Douglas Le Pan, "The Outlook for the Relationship: A Canadian View" in *The United States and Canada*, edited by John Sloan Dickey (Prentice-Hall, Englewood Cliffs, N.J., 1964), p. 165.
2. The *Globe and Mail*, Toronto, July 10, 1971.
3. *The Financial Post*, Toronto, November 13, 1971.

CHAPTER 9

National Interest In Action:
Statesmanship, Policy, Diplomacy

Independence in a community of nations requires considerable toleration of disagreement and effective processes for the accommodation of divergent interests. It is axiomatic that the Canadian neighbor envisaged in the American President's December 1971 reassurances, "not only independent both politically and economically but also one . . . confident that the decisions and policies in each of these sectors would be taken by Canadians in their own interests, in defence of their own values, and in pursuit of their own goals," will frequently put the "clear interests of the United States" in an independent Canada to the test. This testing will measure both the processes for reaching agreement in the affairs of the relationship and the capacity of the United States to tolerate divergences which cannot be readily reconciled.

The sustained pursuit of this somewhat precarious national interest through policy and diplomacy must rest on the judgment that a measure of Canadian divergence is not an aberration but is normal, indeed essential, to a healthy United States-Canada relationship. Above all, perhaps, there must be the American conviction that day-in and day-out political, economic, and defense interests of the United States will fare better in an independent Canada than they would with Canada as a satellite, client state. A judgment of this nature will be more a matter of cumulative comprehension than a specific act of decision.

Whether the United States would have the power, let alone the political will, to coerce Canada into the status of a client state is today the "unthinkable" question. Since 1812, statesmanship on both sides of the border has kept that question from being raised in its ultimate form. Theoretically, in a world of nation states it is conceivable that a day might come when a crisis in America's security would override all other considerations, including the American interest in an independent Canada. All that can usefully be said about such a hypothetical calamity is that the best protection against it is a relationship of mutual trust and confidence that in time of crisis would make the use of American force against Canada as unnecessary as at other times it would be unthinkable.

For the United States today the only real alternative to being guided by an interest in an independent Canada is to be largely unaware and indifferent to the overhang of its presence and policies in Canadian life. Such an alternative simply leaves concern for independent Canadian nationhood outside the scope of American national interest. It projects a course of policy and diplomacy that is more "unthinking" than "unthinkable" and whatever may have been its validity as a form of national interest in an earlier period, it hardly merits analysis as a rational alternative for today's relationship. Suffice for present purposes to say that such has not been the policy premise of contemporary American diplomacy, and it certainly is not compatible with the "fundamental tenet" laid down for United States-Canada relations in the American President's 1971 assurances to Prime Minister Trudeau.

The critical problem for the United States today is to pursue its other national interests through policy and diplomacy without compromising its long-range interest in an independent Canada. It is not uncommon for a nation to be faced with competition between its immediate and its longer-run interests. Such conflicts must be resolved by the hoped-for wisdom of statesmanship and the "fine-tuning" characteristic of good foreign policy and perceptive diplomacy. Inevitably, the sustained pursuit of this long-range interest will generate more conflicts of this nature today than in the past and their resolution both within the United States goverment and with Canada will put special demands on American statesmanship and diplomacy.

Under the best of circumstances the ground between the public perception of the national interest and an internationally negotiated policy is likely to be more strewn with complications and hazards than most critics are permitted to know. On both sides of the border the diplomacy of the United States-Canada relationship may be particularly susceptible to an occupational hazard all diplomats face, namely the predisposition of many politicians, especially in democratic societies, to regard their own foreign policy practitioners as no match for their wily counterparts in other lands. This hazard is especially acute when overtly nationalistic policies are the order of the day. The chronic vulnerability of both United States and Canadian diplomacy to nationalistic criticism is grounded in the acute disparities of power that dominate the relationship: while many Canadians cannot credit their officials with being either able or willing to stand up to behemoth, not a few Americans perceive United States policy and diplomacy as the proverbial elephant paralyzed by the mouse.

Neither of these fears is the prevailing reality. Since Theodore Roosevelt's "big-stick" talk in the Alaska boundary settlement of 1903, American diplomacy has generally eschewed "throwing its weight around" in its relations with Canada. There have been notable exceptions, but it was precisely because the United States policies of August 15, 1971, and Secretary Connally's "diplomacy" were being viewed by many Canadians as drastic departures from past behavior that the Prime Minister thought it necessary to seek presidential reassurances. Yet there is little doubt that policy and diplomacy on both sides of the border have been veering toward a more nationalistic stance. It is not possible yet to know to what extent this development reflects objective interests, nationalistic reaction to the other nation's nationalism and a generally more nationalistic climate throughout the international community. All three are present to some degree, but the prominence of nationalistic reaction to Canada's nationalism is suggested by the increasing frequency with which individuals in American governmental and business circles complain that "the Canadians are getting away with murder," "they want to have it both ways." Whatever the varying merit of such feelings in particular matters, they do reflect a growing assumption by interested Americans that United States policy and diplomacy will harden if the relationship becomes progressively more negative.

There can be genuine perplexity as to how the United States can best respond to Canada's "new nationalism." It will often be a toss-up as to whether a tough policy response is more likely to spread the emotional appeal in Canada of the militant nationalists or to strengthen the position of Canadian moderates by demonstrating that militant policies generate a militant response—a kind of wisdom not instinctive in aroused nationalists on either side of the border who are quick to prefer the retaliatory route.

On the Canadian side, the nationalistic mood puts especially heavy constraints on large-scale collaborative policies. Side by side with a growing sense of national confidence, there is somewhat paradoxically also a resurgence of the underdog's fear of finding himself negotiating on the topdog's terms. This historic wariness is powerfully fortified by the "new nationalism's" view of comprehensive collaboration with the United States as "continentalism," the road in their view to dependence and national suicide. And then there is "August 15, 1971 and all that," as a result of which Peter Dobell, a knowledgeable observer of Canadian foreign affairs, concludes, "Canadian policy toward the United States will never again be as trusting as it had been in the past." Finally, as a matter of official policy, there is the acceptance by the Trudeau Government of the so-called "Third Option" in the trilogy of policy choices expounded in 1972 by then Secretary of State for External Affairs, Mitchell Sharp, whereby Canada now seeks more "diversification" in its foreign relations in order to reduce Canadian vulnerability to "the American impact," particularly in economic affairs.

All of the foregoing, especially the determination to reduce her dependence on the United States, make it unlikely that Canada for the foreseeable future will initiate or welcome policies looking toward substantially greater economic integration in the bilateral relationship. Any significant new policy movement in that direction like the defense alliance that came with World War II and the Cold War, is likely to be more in response to developments in the international community than to essentially bilateral factors in the relationship itself.

Such is the background climate that is likely to prevail in the policy affairs of the relationship for at least the decade of the 1970s. It is marginal "see and be seen" flying weather, but it is far from a ceiling zero condition. It is a period in the relationship that will require genuinely wise American statesmanship and extraordinary skill in the nation's diplomacy if sterile, even destructive, confrontations are to be avoided or at least held to a minimum. An interest in having Canada independent of the United States receives little critical scrutiny so long as the normal competitive interests of the two countries are being pursued within the cushioning collaboration of an expanding relationship. When that context is lacking or called in question, nationalistic considerations tend to force all policy disagreements into the unduly rigid framework of dilemmas requiring a choice as between immediate and longer-range interests. In the near years ahead, the relationship will face the need to manage such dilemmas in energy, investment, trade, and cultural relations; conceivably also in continental defense.

No subject on the agenda of the decade promises greater difficulty than that complex of perplexities designated "the energy crisis." For at least the balance of the 1970s, the short supply and cost exigencies of oil and gas, will create profound problems in the international as well as the domestic affairs of the two countries. Both nations have a high per capita energy consumption, but on the supply side Canada is potentially self-sufficient for at least several decades, while the United

States faces increasing dependence on foreign sources, unprecedented cost levels, possibly crippling shortages and, at best, difficult and unpopular conservation measures.

Superficially, this may suggest that the old saw about Canada getting pneumonia when the United States sneezes is about to be reversed. In fact, the outcome may be a new experience in the realities of interdependence. A prolonged American recession induced or aggravated by an extended energy crisis, with its inevitable repercussions on the Canadian economy, could make Canada's energy self-sufficiency cold comfort indeed. The 1973-74 onset of the energy crisis aroused nationalistic reactions in both countries that will aggravate all policy problems for some time, but in the longer run the emotional luxury of such sentiments will likely be subordinated to economic realities. Despite the immediate instinct of both societies to seek security in energy self-sufficiency, it is probably prudent policy to reckon with the possibility that ultimately shared self-interest may make more collaborative policies attractive.

However the interface of the relationship on energy develops, three fundamentals will be involved: (1) supply, (2) conservation, and (3) national attitudes.

In 1973 an official Canadian analysis summarized the supply situation as follows:

> While Canada is self-sufficient in terms of energy production it does not have the potential to play a major role with regard to total North American needs. Our present exports to the United States meet less than 6 percent of that country's oil and gas requirements ... but do play an important role in providing secure supply and in meeting a large portion of the needs of specific regional markets. Future oil and gas exports from Canada to the United States or to new export markets will depend heavily on the success of frontier oil exploration and new production technology for the oil sands. Conceivably Canada's contribution to total U.S. oil and gas needs in the year 2000 could range from zero to 12 per cent.

Canada is dependent on the United States for about 20 million tons of coal imports for Ontario needs. Over the years, the two nations have been more or less in balance on electrical energy trade. In 1972 there was a net electrical energy export from Canada equal to 3.3 percent of total Canadian generation which represented about one half of 1 percent of United States needs. . . . We are fortunate in having an assured energy resource self-sufficiency for a long period in the future, but Canada's future role as a world energy source will not be significant.[1]

The Supply Outlook

Later assessments of Canada's energy outlook are more cautious. As of early 1975, the United States is on notice that it cannot expect exports of oil from Canada to continue after 1982. The near prospect is that by 1976 Canadian oil exports will have been curtailed to between 650 to 800 barrels per day from the million plus barrels exported daily in 1972. Additional supplies of gas and hydro power are somewhat more likely, but the prospect is that these and other energy exports will be subject to stringent reservations regarding Canada's right to terminate. Depending upon the changing calculation of future Canadian supplies and needs, there may be theoretically some room for Canada to trade off something from her long-range oil and gas reserves for other benefits. Practical and political considerations are such, however, that such assistance on the supply side in the near future would likely be more important psychologically than materially. In the longer run, probably by the mid-80s, there is a more realistic prospect of increased Canadian oil supplies from a successful exploitation of the Athabaska oil sands and the possibility of new oil and gas discoveries in the Arctic and off the east coast. Likewise there are substantial new hydro power potentialities in Quebec's James Bay, in Manitoba, and perhaps a decade or so later from the tides of Fundy. There is also increasing interest in Canada's long-range potential as a producer of an exportable surplus of nuclear-generated power, particularly in the Atlantic provinces. The optimum development of all such possibilities, however, will involve massive inputs of capital, technology, management, patience in the resolution of critical ecological issues, along with extraordinary political wisdom and leadership. The need for creative collaboration as between Ottawa and the provinces, externally with the United States, and by the governments with private enterprise in both countries would be unprecedented. Above all, the large-scale development of new sources of exportable Canadian energy will require a perception of shared self-interest in the interdependence of the two societies that is not present today.

Too many fundamental factors are as yet unclear or undecided to permit any exact forecast of the capital investment that might be needed to bring Canada's energy resources to optimum development. The magnitude can be suggested. Dr. Suleyman Sarpkaya, economic adviser to the Canadian bankers association, has estimated that Canada's energy industries would need 95 billion dollars (in 1971 dollars) for new capital projects in the 1971-1985 period.[2] As of 1975, a ten-year projection of the capital requirements for energy development is upwards of a $115 billion range.[3] Estimates of net external capital requirements suggest that perhaps a fourth to a third of such needs would need to come from outside Canada.[4]

Estimates for particular projects provide a more meaningful view of the unprecedented magnitude of certain projects. The largest and probably the most relevant to the United States interest is the proposal for a Mackenzie Valley gas pipeline extending 2,600 miles from the Arctic to the United States border, at an estimated cost in 1974 of about 6 billion dollars. This project, planned by Canadian Arctic Gas Study Limited, a consortium of Canadian and American interests, has had strong encouragement from the Canadian government. The financing of this gigantic undertaking, said to be the largest single construction project in the world, is regarded as manageable, assuming there is an adequate supply of natural gas to provide the transportation of 30 trillion cubic feet over the twenty year normal life of the projected 48-inch line. As late as 1974, such a future supply from Canadian sources was far from being a certainty. To meet this critical need, the Trudeau Government undertook a strong initiative to interest the

United States in bringing Alaska's Prudhoe Bay gas out through Canada *via* a Mackenzie Delta line. In 1974, Mr. Donald Macdonald, Minister of Energy, Mines and Resources, met a "scrupulously noncommital" reception in Washington,[5] but discussions continue on a combined project now estimated at 10 billion dollars.

The negotiation of such an arrangement presents major difficulties. On the American side, there is the *sine qua non* to have firm assurances regarding secure transit for American gas via a pipeline located in Canada. It now seems likely that a treaty providing reciprocal transit assurances for all United States-Canada transnational pipelines will be negotiated. There is also powerful business opposition in the United States from the El Paso Natural Gas Company which advocates paralleling the new Prudhoe Bay oil line with a gas line across Alaska. On the Canadian side, there will be the need both to protect future Canadian gas needs and to assure Canadian control of the project to avoid an affront to nationalistic concerns. The magnitude of the external capital requirements will inevitably be controversial. Moreover, there is an urgent time factor which may not be compatible with the long drawn out regulatory processes now under way in both countries.

The major presently known potential for additional Canadian oil is the Athabaska tar sands in northeastern Alberta. This potential has been under experimental development for over 15 years, but the 1973 crisis in oil supplies and the ensuing revolution in prices greatly heightened interest in it. Although estimates vary considerably, the tar sands are reputed to contain recoverable reserves of 75 to 80 billion barrels with existing technology and with the *in situ* technology envisaged for the more distant future, estimates go much higher. Great Canadian Oil Sands Ltd., controlled by the Sun Oil Company of Pennsylvania, after six years of experimenting achieved a limited commercial production of about 50,000 barrels a day in 1973. Syncrude Canada, Ltd., originally a consortium of American controlled Canadian oil companies, which had hoped to have a plant producing by 1978, ran into severe financial troubles in 1974 caused by the prospect of a doubling of the capital requirements. The project, after the withdrawal of Atlantic Richfield as a principal participant, was rescued by the decision of the Canadian government and the governments of Alberta and Ontario to put up 600 million dollars of the necessary capital.

The present strip-mining technology is expected to produce 110 to 125,000 barrels a day on an estimated investment that has climbed in several years from 750 million to 2,000 million dollars. Earlier it was estimated that production from the oil sands by the early 1980s could be between 400,000 to 500,000 barrels a day and in early 1974 Gulf Oil, a participant in the Syncrude consortium, reported estimates that by 1985 maximum production from the tar sands could be as high as 1,250,000 barrels daily.[6] The subsequent crisis in this and other pending projects caused by the escalation of capital requirements has probably largely invalidated such estimates. Manifestly, the price of oil internationally will be a major factor governing the future development of this inescapably expensive source of new oil. The magnitude of the uncertainties involved is illustrated by the fact that as recently as 1973 the Continental Oil Co. estimated that with an investment of 200 million dollars for the mine, 550 million dollars for the processing plant and 3.55 dollars operating cost per barrel, the f.o.b. plant price per barrel of syncrude in 1978 would be 8.70 dollars. Estimates by other oil authorities in 1974 projected a price per barrel in the 10- to 11-dollar range, assuming capital investment of about 1 billion dollars to produce 125,000 barrels per day; by 1975 the estimated capital requirement had doubled.

Between the theoretical potential for thus increasing Canada's oil supply and its realization there are also such formidable hurdles as environmental concerns (today's mining requires two tons of sand for one barrel of oil), uncertainty as to both federal and provincial policies on financing, taxes, licensing for export, royalties, and the possibility of new competing energy sources before the investment has paid out.

Within the next decade the proposed Mackenzie Valley gas pipeline and the all-out development of the tar sands could require upwards of 20 billion dollars. It is certain that there would be a strong emphasis on using internally generated Canadian capital and Canadian content in all forms wherever possible. Consideration of the Mackenzie Valley gas line has long presumed at least 51 percent Canadian control of the equity, and Minister Macdonald has repeatedly cautioned against any expectation that Canada would welcome massive American investment in the development of the oil sands. Indeed, it is certain, as Prime Minister Trudeau forecast in the 1974 election campaign, the extension of American control of Canadian natural resources will not be welcomed.

Canadian control of such natural resource developments need not, of course, preclude the utilization of foreign capital in forms and amounts short of ownership control. The earlier hydro power development in Labrador and Quebec's current James Bay project, the overall cost estimates for which now range from 9 to 12 billion dollars are instances of Canadian energy developments requiring immense amounts of foreign debt capital. It has already proved impossible to arrange the vast financing needed for development of the tar sands without governmental participation and under any foreseeable circumstances, in one form or another, the future role of government in such gigantic energy developments will presumably either be dominant enough or sufficiently influential to assure that the ownership control is Canadian. Even so, there will be many financial perplexities to be settled in both the private and public sectors before a new multibillion gas pipeline and a large flow of tar sands oil are realities in Canada.

Manifestly, the wise management of the financial, trade and manpower components in such out-sized development projects will involve governmental attention to the impact on major national interests, especially the balance of payments and exchange rates. The magnitude of financing is such that many areas of the Canadian economy would be affected and the impact would be great on the economic relations of the two countries. The policy trade offs could be quite fundamental. For example, a Canadian student of industrial organization and energy economics, Professor Leonard Waverman, has warned against pushing economic nationalism too far in the financing of the gas pipeline:

. . . a requirement of 100% domestic financing of the
pipeline could have as its only impact an increase in
foreign investment in other sectors of the Canadian
economy. I would rather see foreign investment in a
pipeline regulated under federal jurisdiction than see it
in unregulated areas of the Canadian economy.[7]

One of the "dividends" of the oil crisis of 1973 was the
demonstration that extensive foreign investment in large enterprises is no match for resolute, resourceful government
policy by a host country. Canada's resort to a tax on her oil
exports to the United States in managing domestic price levels
may in retrospect suggest that, when the "chips are down,"
host governments are not as powerless to deal with multinational enterprises as some of their critics have proclaimed.
More realistic confidence in the regulatory resourcefulness of
modern governments may even—*mirabile dictu*—come to be
regarded by the multinationals as the ultimate answer to nationalistic ideologues.

Canada's future potential for producing hydro energy is also
present in the perennial Bay of Fundy tidal scheme. With
today's new energy costs this idea may not be as unrealistic as
once thought and fresh studies of it are being launched. In
April 1973 a published esimate put the cost of the project at $2
billion for a 3,700 megawatt facility,[8] an estimate that is at
least several times too low even today.[9] A Canadian financial
authority who studied the subject at an earlier stage has expressed the private judgment that its feasibility both economically and technologically is at least another decade off.

Along with such long-range projects that might provide
Canada with more exportable energy, there is an imminent
development that will reduce the availability of Canadian oil
for export to the United States. The 1973 international oil
crisis persuaded the Trudeau Government to abandon Canada's policy of relying on imported oil for eastern Canada's
needs (about half of the national requirements), and instead
to begin making Canada's potential self-sufficiency a reality by
extending the existing pipeline carrying western oil from its
present terminus at Sarnia, Ontario, to Montreal. The 250,000

barrels per day needed for this projected line, which is
scheduled for completion by late 1976, would presumably
come out of Canada's current exports to American Middle-
West refineries, which for the last six month's of 1975 is
authorized at 750,000 barrels daily.

Shared Conservation and Understanding

Any sustained concern with the energy supply problem
must also reckon with the need of both nations to develop
effective, harmonious conservation programs. Their inter-
locked economic well-being, their high stakes in an essentially
integrated automobile industry with its special interest in
some 70 million annual transborder crossings that daily put
the common life styles of the two societies on exhibit, make it
unlikely that Canada and the United States could long tolerate great divergence as between them in their private practises
and public policies on anything as basic to their common
welfare as the conservation of energy during an extended supply crisis. The reality of this possibility for trouble is witnessed
by a recent editorial complaint from Vermont, asking "Can
anyone remember passing a Canadian driver on the interstate
recently? Probably not but we'll bet you can recall the reverse!
Now we have nothing against the good neighbors to the
North. However, many of them drive through this area as if
there were no tomorrow and no energy crisis. . . . This isn't to
suggest a vendetta against Canadian drivers but if a few were
sufficiently inconvenienced by having to answer speeding
charges so far from home, the word might carry across the
border."[10] A collaborative approach to energy conservation
could help to moderate nationalistic exacerbation and keep
popular misunderstandings at a minimum.

National emotions and attitudes will be severely tested by
an extended period of shortages and high prices. In 1973,
nationalistic umbrage toward Canada quickly appeared in
Congress and the American press; President Nixon noted
publicly that even the "friendly Canadians" could be difficult.
Mr. Trudeau's public reassurance that Canada had no thought
of withholding from the United States any energy supplies
that could be spared had to compete with more nationalistic

uttcrances and it was subsequently largely lost in the controversies stirred by Canada's tax on oil exports and the short-fall of contract gas from British Columbia.

In a perverse but instructive way, history may be repeating itself. During the early crisis years of both World Wars, many hard-pressed Canadians found America's comfortable non-involvement difficult to understand and accept. A prolonged energy crisis with its reversed scenario and compounded by Canada's "new nationalism" will assuredly generate comparable feelings in the United States.

Neither nation can afford the indulgence of self-satisfied indifference or petulant recrimination. What can be done concretely is beyond prescription here. Ultimately, nothing less than a lease kind of creative collaboration may be necessary, but whatever exigencies may lie ahead, a fundamental first step that might now also be both psychologically reassuring to Americans and politically acceptable to Canadians would be the creation of a joint clearing house for a continuous, systematic exchange on energy conservation and the related environmental issues which will become increasingly acute as the pressure builds for new sources of supply.

Canada's energy development and foreign investment grew up together. From the 1950s on, Canada's energy and mineral resources attracted foreign investment on a scale that taken with the already burgeoning American presence in manufacturing generated a major new nationalistic concern in Canadian life. Now it is likely that the policy offspring of that concern, Canada's new Foreign Investment Review Agency, will be far more involved with the international perplexities of the energy crisis than anyone foresaw in 1973 when, after twenty years of searching for an acceptable policy, Canada decided to screen foreign take-overs, new investment and business expansion into "unrelated" fields against the "significant benefit" to Canada of the proposed foreign investment. Prior to energy's sudden rise to the status of trump in international affairs, Canada's growing concern about the extent of American investment in her industries promised to be essentially a domestic issue requiring more diplomacy in reconciling federal-provincial views than United States-Canada disagreements. The impact of the energy crisis is likely to change the prospect by introducing large new dimensions of international governmental interest and concern, particularly on the part of the United States. Increasingly these concerns will touch the entire range of international financial and trade policies. And even in the regulation of foreign direct investment, especially in energy related ventures, testing projects for "significant benefit" to Canada is likely to be matched by a corresponding concern for "significant benefit" to the United States. Under these circumstances, the foreign investment policies of both countries will increasingly influence the foreign policies of the two countries and the future of the relationship.

The outlook for United States-Canada trade policies will also be importantly influenced by the manner in which the energy crisis is met by the two countries. Highly nationalistic policies on energy would tend to propagate similar policies in trade matters. On the other hand, if the two countries find common ground and significant collaborative approaches in energy, such collaboration will perforce involve trade policies both directly and indirectly. Prior to the oil embargo crisis of late 1973, Canada's unwillingness to discuss anything remotely suggesting a continental approach to energy was matched by the unwillingness of certain American officials to contemplate even the possibility of a linkage between Canada's energy resources and Canada's need for assured access for Canadian trade in the American market. Nothing resembling a comprehensive free trade arrangement is currently of interest to either country, but it is at least open to question whether failure to explore possible linkages between energy, foreign investment and trade policies will long be compatible with the welfare of either country. Unless and until nationalistic ceilings on such policy initiatives are raised, trade flow in the relationship is likely to remain a hostage to the energy crisis even though both countries are seeking further trade liberalization through multilateral negotiations under GATT auspices. If, unhappily, world economic conditions, including the energy crisis, should develop unfavorably for these negotiations, continuation of the liberal inclination of United

States trade policy during the past forty years is far from assured by the 1974 Trade Reform Act which, while primarily aimed at trade liberalization, also includes broad grants of power capable of unilateral restrictive use. In this respect, this legislation is probably less a commitment to liberal trade policies than the initial Trade Agreements Act of 1934. Depending upon a particular administration's perception of the national interest (international commitments aside), the 1974 Act could be almost as powerful a weapon of trade warfare as of trade liberalization—its passing "bow" to the idea of U.S.-Canada free trade not withstanding.

No catastrophic threat to the world's largest bilateral trading relationship impends, but neither is the future of the trade relationship assured by policies and processes in place today. Canada's livelihood requires the export of about half in value of all the goods she produces and Canadian nationhood requires progressively larger programs of industrial development to employ a growing labor force and to reduce the disintegrating forces of her regional disparities. However successful her long-range efforts to develop greater "diversification" in her foreign relations, there is no foreseeable prospect of Canada being willing or able to reduce her exports and imports in the United States relationship much below the steady state level of more than two thirds of her total trade.

A prolonged period of reciprocating nationalistic restrictions during the next decade could change this outlook but only at great cost to the general health as well as the economic welfare of the relationship. The first tangible evidence that an independent Canada is at best a dispensable United States national interest would likely take the form of a progressive indifference in American official and private attitudes to having Canada "hurt a little more." Such an attitude led in 1866 to termination by the United States of more than a decade of reciprocity, a step that cast seventy years of shadow on the trading relationship of the two countries.

In recent decades, the continuing growth of trade and investment made large, collaborative policy approaches seem unnecessary as well as undesirable (except for the *sui generis* Auto Pact) to both nations. Today such growth is increasingly a matter of national concern, both positively and negatively, to the two governments. Almost certainly it will not be left as free of governmental influence as in the past, but the extent to which that influence will involve new collaborative ventures can only be answered by statesmanship.

Whether the energy crisis is sufficiently *sui generis* in its impact on the interdependent well being of the two countries to create a new climate for collaborative processes and policies will likely be revealed well before the end of the 1970s. The underlying realities of the crisis will not go away in that time and inescapably the two governments will make specific policy decisions that will add up to a relationship either more collaborative or more nationalistic in its approach to the future.

No background factor will influence such large choices more than the temper of Canadian nationalism. During this period of spreading nationalistic concerns, both cultural and economic, the prime target of political action will be the conspicuous American business presence. Even if Canada's regulation of foreign investment is able to avoid the touchy issues of retroactive or discriminatory application, its operation at least in some important instances will involve bargaining with American enterprises over terms and conditions to a point where a counter concern on the part of the U.S. Government is likely to be generated. And beyond the screening operation, existing U.S. controlled enterprises will likely be the subject of increasing critical scrutiny, as recently evidenced by: the decision to withdraw the domestic status under the Income Tax Law enjoyed by the Canadian editions of *Time* and *Reader's Digest*, the proposal to prohibit compliance by businesses in Canada with the United States Trading-with-the-Enemy Act, and the readiness of the Trudeau Government on occasion to bring individual American controlled enterprises before the bar of public opinion on the issue of "good Canadian citizenship."

Several instances are instructive with respect to the changing postures of two governments on these aspects of the American business presence. The first, which arose in 1974, involved the United States Trading-with-the-Enemy Act and a Canadian manufacturing firm, 52 percent owned by the

American parent concern, Studebaker-Worthington, proposing to sell 30 locomotives to the Cuban government, a transaction that under United States law would have been forbidden an American company. The controlling American corporate owner sought an exemption for the transaction from the Treasury, which passed the issue on to the State Department. The issue quickly became a public controversy in Canada, with the Trudeau Government taking an adamant position that one way or another the sale would be carried out; and eventually it was. The State Department apparently concluding, wisely it would seem, that this was neither the time nor the issue for a confrontation with Canada. Several similar exemptions have since been granted.

Leaving aside the underlying question of attempting to proscribe "trading-with-the-enemy" in the hemisphere in a time of United States-Soviet détente, an issue of this nature creates in today's Canada a public-political eruption which like the Mercantile Bank case in the 1960s spreads the hot lava of nationalistic indignation from coast to coast. The predictable public and official reaction was that the time had come for foreign controlled Canadian companies to be unambiguously free of any need to comply with such requirements of foreign law, and proposals to that end have been introduced in Parliament.

1973 and its energy crisis produced one of the rare cases of a Canadian Minister taking an American corporation's subsidiary to task on the floor of the House of Commons for "bad corporate citizenship." On November 1, 1973, the Canadian Minister of Energy, Mines and Resources, Donald Macdonald, stated in the House his appreciation to the oil industry, "with one notable exception, for the cooperation that has been evident from them . . . in keeping Canadian prices down. The notable exception is Gulf Canada." Mr. Macdonald then pointedly added in reference to a proposal for raising prices by the president of the subsidiary, "this American president of that American corporation has set this House a good example of bad corporate citizenship."[11] Without venturing into the merits of the matter, the Minister's emphasis on the American identification *per se* reveals the increasingly marginal acceptance under which American enterprises must often be prepared to operate.

Less conspicuous and presently far less controversial than the American business presence but no less a potential policy problem in the future is the continental defense alliance under NORAD which in May 1975 was renewed for five years subject to termination on a year's notice. Short of some unforeseen catastrophic upheaval in the relationship, this important collaboration seems stabilized for some years but as observed in Chapter 4, it is an area of the relationship that is always potentially vulnerable to an aroused nationalism. It is a policy area where long-range United States interests counsel patience, sensitivity to Canada's sensitivity, and a not-too-anxious posture.

Over all, as the two nations today seek policies more attuned to immediate, readily perceptible national interests, more abstract interests become suspect. The reality of the American interest in an independent Canada is peculiarly vulnerable to such discounting: its future will depend basically on a more profound American understanding of this interest as well as wise statesmanship and skillful diplomacy in both countries.

. An independent Canada neither needs nor should expect to meet a soft, complaisant United States. Even though some issues may arouse strong opposition in Canada, where the United States thinks it has the better case it assuredly should and will seek to prevail. Aside from the adverse reaction a feckless diplomacy would generate in the United States, any form of American paternalism could quickly give Canadian independence the *coup de grâce*. The point was made by A. E. Ritchie, then Undersecretary of State for External Affairs, before a committee of the Canadian Parliament on May 5, 1970. He noted that in United States-Canadian negotiations the expectation of favors was unrealistic and would mean "risking our independence in a way that I think we do not risk it when we negotiate a pretty hard-headed bargain on a particular point."

The issue here is not one of favors, paternalism, soft negotiations, suppression of dissatisfactions and a fantasy of bland

politeness between the two societies. Rather, it is the ability of
the United States in its enlightened self-interest to live and
work and disagree, without petulance or retaliatory posturing,
with a Canada which on occasion will diverge from the policies
of the United States in the conduct of her foreign affairs, and
which for a long time to come will be an uneasy neighbor. The
important truth for both nations to perceive and practice is
that this is one of those twilight areas of statecraft where great
consequences may turn on judgment and differences of degree: for Canada, in the way she distinguishes between the
rigorous assertion of legitimate American interests and the
remote possibility of being "pushed around" on her national
policies or blackguarded for a divergent initiative; for the
United States, in the self-discipline of asserting its interests
through policies and a diplomacy which are compatible with
its encompassing national interest in having a neighbor which,
while far less powerful, is neither pusillanimous nor paranoid.

In point of fact, although there have been perhaps a dozen
or so major disagreements during the past several decades,
there have been singularly few instances where responsible
Canadian authorities have felt seriously aggrieved by unacceptable heavy-handedness on the part of American diplomacy. Even in the sensitive area of the American direct
investment presence, the Gray Report found little evidence of
worrisome intervention by the United States government in
the protection of American business interests, the only two
cases cited being the Mercantile Bank and the *Time-Reader's
Digest* controversies of the early 1960s.

The probability of really dangerous policy divergence by an
independent Canada is, in fact, not very great. Prime Minister
Trudeau, although uneasy about bedding down with the elephant, even in a continental-sized bed, put it realistically:

> . . . there is bound to be always a preoccupation in
> Canada with whether we're doing something which
> makes sense in United States terms, just because of our
> long relationships, our history, because of geo-politics,
> because of friendship, because of relatives which we have
> on both sides of the border, because of business connec-

tions, but basically I think because of geo-politics. It's just nonsense to think that when we are a large land mass with a rather small population next to the most powerful nation in the world, that we're not going to be constantly influenced by and preoccupied with the feelings down there.[12]

Yes and no but on the record, still mainly yes.

Notes

1. *An Energy Policy for Canada*, Summary of Analysis, Issued under authority of the Minister of Energy, Mines and Resources, 1973, pp. 16-17.
2. *Financial Post*, Toronto, April 28, 1973.
3. *Financial Post*, Toronto, April 26, 1975, fourth sec; pp. D1-D8.
4. *Financial Post*, Toronto, October 28, 1972 (A.B. Hockin).
5. *New York Times*, February 2, 1974, p. 37.
6. Special Issue of *The Orange Disc*, March-April 1974, p. 7.
7. *Financial Post*, Toronto, April 28, 1973, p. 39.
8. *Financial Post*, Toronto, April 28, 1973, p. 36.
9. *Financial Post*, Toronto, April 26, 1975, p. D3.
10. *The Valley News*, White River Junction, Vermont, May 8, 1975.
11. *International Canada*, November 1973, p. 287.
12. Unpublished interview with James Reston in December 1971; text published by the Canadian Embassy in Washington, D.C.

CHAPTER 10

The Relationship and The Hemisphere: The O.A.S. Question

Canada's search for diversification, coupled with the global interests of the United States, will increasingly bring bilateral United States-Canada policies under the influence of developments outside the relationship itself. These two centrifugal forces are already producing this result in the Western Hemisphere. The potential for significant change in the bilateral relationship is inherent in Canada's increasing interest in hemispheric affairs, especially in the perplexing question of her relationship to the Organization of American States (O.A.S.). No issue better illustrates the way in which the United States interests in an independent Canada can come into conflict with other strongly held United States interests.

The O.A.S. question has a considerable history. Up until just prior to World War II, the United States had an ingrained negative attitude toward any thought of Canadian membership in the Pan American Union, the predecessor organization of the O.A.S. In fact, the possibility of an organic relationship to the American republics on the part of Canada was long regarded in United States diplomatic circles as constitutionally incompatible with Canada's status as a kingdom and dominion of the British Empire. Needless to say, there were also strong Monroe Doctrine overtones in this view of the matter.

Shortly before war broke out in 1939, the American attitude began to change and the possibility of Canadian membership was tentatively raised, but Prime Minister King felt that the time for it was not ripe. At the time some attributed Canada's attitude to "fear of compromising her position in the British family of nations." [1] And yet today with that fear gone and after pondering the question of O.A.S. membership for a quarter of a century, Canada has still not found the time ripe. It seems quite likely that, as in so many other situations, Mackenzie King may have given a polite negative rather than the real one, i.e., a concern not to overload the Canada-United States relationship with unnecessary risks of trouble. This concern continues.

From time to time individual Canadian officials have indicated a positive interest in O.A.S. membership. In 1967 Paul Martin, during his service as Secretary of State for External Affairs in the Pearson Government, predicted that "membership in the O.A.S. is part of the ultimate destiny of Canada as a country of the Western Hemisphere"; in 1972, while leader of the Government in the Senate, Mr. Martin felt that complications arising from O.A.S. membership were becoming "less and less likely."

In 1968, prior to becoming Prime Minister, Mr. Trudeau, with a candor that has generally characterized his personal statements on foreign affairs, conditioned his support for eventual O.A.S. membership on Canada's being ready and able to act independently of the United States on hemispheric issues. Two years later, however, his Government's White Paper, *Foreign Policy for Canadians*, was significantly more guarded. While proposing the active extension of Canadian interests in Latin American and the Caribbean, this policy review avoided mention of the "U.S. factor" in discussing the O.A.S. question. Although the issue of full membership was left in carefully considered limbo, the White Paper foresaw the possibility of Canadian participation in O.A.S. affairs in other forms.

In 1972 the O.A.S., eager to have as much Canadian participation as possible, created the position of nonvoting Permanent Observer. Canada was admitted in that capacity in April of that year. A month later Canada further extended its hemispheric connections by becoming a member of the Inter-American Development Bank, a step that quickly gave substance to apprehensions about possible confrontations with the United States in O.A.S. affairs.

At the time Canada accepted Permanent Observer status, the influential Toronto *Globe and Mail* observed:

> Canada has long resisted joining the OAS, largely because it was a United States-dominated organization in which Canada would either have to buckle under the U.S. decisions—such as the invasion of the Dominican Republic—and thereby be seen to be a flunky of our powerful neighbor, or be in constant and probably useless conflict with one of our closest allies and best customers.[2]

Some favored full membership, but others, including the *Ottawa Citizen*, while recognizing that many Latin American countries "would prefer Canada's full entry . . . partly as a counterweight to the United States," supported observer status as "useful enough." [3]

Manifestly, the balance must be struck by Canada as to where her interest lies. But the matter has also become a question of United States policy, inasmuch as it has repeatedly encouraged Canada to accept the responsibilities of full O.A.S. membership. The issue provides an unusually instructive case history of potentially divergent United States national interests.

The United States played the leading role in the transformation in 1948 of the somewhat amorphous Pan American Union into the more structurally developed Organization of American States. The new setup, which had strong Latin American support, was clearly designed to accommodate Canadian membership. Since then, as an American scholar, John Plank, observed, it has been "almost an article of faith, in the United States, that at some juncture Canada will become a member . . . [although] like most articles of faith, this one is seldom subjected to critical scrutiny." [4]

On May 17, 1961, the desirability of Canadian membership was officially, even fulsomely, blessed by President Kennedy in an address to the Canadian Parliament. The President's words, which were more in accord with the views of White House advisers than with those of the State Department's experts on Canada, carried the clear message throughout Canada as to what the United States wanted:

> So let us fix our attention not on those matters that vex us as neighbors but on the issues that face us as leaders. Let us look southward as part of the hemisphere with whose fate we are both inextricably bound.
>
> First, consider our mutual hopes for this hemisphere . . . To make this entire area more secure against aggression of all kinds, to defend it against the encroachment of international communism in this hemisphere, and to see our sister states fulfill their hopes and needs of economic and social reform and development are surely all challenges confronting your nation, and deserving of your talents and resources, as well as ours.
>
> To be sure, it would mean an added responsibility; but yours is not a nation that shrinks from responsibility. The hemisphere is a family into which we were born, and we cannot turn our backs on it in time of trouble. Nor can we stand aside from its great adventure of development. I believe that all the free members of the Organization of American States would be heartened and strengthened by any increase in your hemispheric role. Your skills, your resources, your judicious perception at the council table—even when it differs from our own view—are all needed througout the inter-American community. Your country and mine are partners in North American affairs. Can we not now become partners in inter-American affairs? [5]

At the time of President Kennedy's speech, Canada was already experiencing a renaissance of nationalistic feeling under Prime Minister Diefenbaker. And just a month before, the Bay of Pigs fiasco had made many Canadians thankful that they were not closely linked to United States hemispheric policies. It is hardly surprising, therefore, that President Kennedy's appeal to "become partners in inter-American affairs" received a poor reception in Canada. What was surprising was that the President and his White House advisers (who unfortunately were more expert on Latin America than Canada), and apparently the Canadian ambassador in Washington, A. D. P. Heeney, were insensitive to the adverse Canadian reaction such an appeal was likely to arouse. Indeed, it is probable that the reaction stirred by President Kennedy's remarks contributed to Canada's determined divergence on Cuban policy, which in turn later helped encourage certain O.A.S. countries to reexamine their position on Cuba's ostracism.

President Nixon and his advisers were not deterred, however, by the 1961 turndown. A decade later, on April 14, 1972, while eschewing the earlier appeal for help to defend the hemisphere against the encroachment of communism, an American President once again invoked the vision of "partnership within the Western Hemisphere," affirming that "the great community of the Americas cannot be complete without the participation of Canada. . . . That is why we have been encouraged by recent decisions of Canada to upgrade its participation as an observer in the Organization of American States to ambassadorial status, and to apply for membership in the Inter-American Development Bank." Secretary of State Rogers made the American expectation of yet greater participation very explicit in his words of welcome to Canada as a Permanent Observer at the 1972 General Assembly of the O.A.S.: "We look forward to even closer ties between them [Canada and Guyana] and this organization."

American specialists on Latin America have increasingly come to regard the vast disparity in economic strength, national power, and world responsibilities between the United States and the nations to the south as the most fundamental, perhaps the unsurmountable, barrier to satisfactory, genuinely cooperative relations with these nations. The O.A.S. is the institutional embodiment of the problem. At least since F.D.R.'s good-neighbor policy of the 1930s, the United States in a plethora of ways, with varying intensity and several aberrations, has sought with very modest success to minimize or circumvent the problem of United States-Latin American disparities and disagreements. Today this effort continues with a new counsel of realism: "it is not unnatural or unexpected that we should have specific and recurring differences," a view of hemispheric relations somewhat akin to that of the United States in an independent Canada. As explained by Secretary of State Rogers to the O.A.S. General Assembly in April, 1972, "these differences themselves prove the independence and sovereignty of each member state which are so essential to the kind of relationship we desire and so essential to the strength of this organization and its future."

Leaving aside the currently muted notion that Canada should join in a hemispheric defense against communism, any American case for pressing greater O.A.S. responsibilities on Canada would naturally enough include geography and the potential Canadian assets mentioned by President Kennedy in 1961: "Your skills, your resources, your judicious perception at the council table. . . ." A critical scrutiny of the American position, however, can hardly escape doubt that these potential contributions are not the entire inventory of interests behind either the United States or the Latin American desire for a larger Canadian presence in O.A.S. affairs.

Some scholars have concluded that for now and the foreseeable future Canadian membership in the O.A.S. is "an American solution for an American problem." [6] The critical question for American policy is whether the limited contribution Canada could make to coping with hemisphere problems would be overshadowed by the increased burdens on United States-Canada relationship that one way or another are certain to result.

Given Canada's geographic eligibility, her bicultural national character, her developing hemispheric interests, and especially her historic and inherent need for independence vis-à-vis the United States, it is natural enough to think of her membership in the O.A.S. as a potential, albeit limited, answer to the "American problem." And since other American states want Canada in the O.A.S. for their own purposes—as a potential champion and partial offset to United States influence—it might readily seem to be a good fit all around. Parenthetically, it should also be noted that American opposition to Canada's affiliation with the O.A.S. would have created its own special kind of trouble for the United States in both Latin America and Canada.

The question of full O.A.S. membership is now Canada's to decide. Inescapably, that decision raises the question of what such a step might mean for the critical national interests of the United States and Canada in the good health of their bilateral relationship. The possibility clearly cannot be ruled out that full Canadian participation in the O.A.S. might dangerously overload the relationship with difficulties it is poorly prepared at present to bear. If one judges this danger to be substantial, pressing O.A.S. membership on Canada (over and beyond not opposing it) can well be regarded as placing a higher value on a dubious contribution to the United States problems in Latin America than on the nation's stake in maintaining optimum health in its relationship with Canada. At the very least, a considered judgment must be made as to whether the possibilities for prejudicing the bilateral relationship are not greater at this point than is the potential for improvement in inter-American relations through full Canadian involvement.

Historical and geopolitical considerations make it likely, as indeed certain Latin American states assume, that Canada would often find herself unable to avoid the role of the balancing weight on a hemispheric teeter-totter, with the United States on the "heavy minority" side of many issues. The developing nations everywhere and, of course, the communist nations, would follow such occasions closely for a reading on Canada's independence of the United States interest and influence. In situations where the Canadian interest coincided with the American position, e.g., expropriation issues, frequent support for the United States would be certain to diminish the quality of Canadian independence in the eyes of many in the international community. The O.A.S. is of course, much more vulnerable to this type of trouble than larger, more balanced forums such as the United Nations or even NATO.

Support for the United States positions also would certainly be watched very suspiciously by nationalists in Canada. The likelihood is that such support would be used to keep the home fires of anti-Americanism burning—a prospect not to be taken lightly, especially during a period when both governments are understandably anxious not to have either their own or the other nation's nationalism get out of hand.

It also bears consideration that what is involved is far from being an all-or-nothing issue. It is one thing for Canada as a nonvoting Permanent Observer to be able to select on an *ad hoc* basis the hemispheric issues on which it wishes to become involved, informally or otherwise, and quite another to be required by the responsibilities of full membership to pass on all O.A.S. issues under the spotlight of publicity that plays on the proceedings of an international organization.

There is also the United States domestic situation to consider. Canadian-American divergences within international organizations, particularly if the United States is on the losing side, tend to get much more critical attention in the United States than most bilateral disagreements. It is partly the greater public aspect of issues in an international organization, and partly the political drama involved in being publicly voted down by one's closest neighbor, ally, and, as we so readily proclaim, "partner." The American public and the American Congress have come a considerable way in recent years in accepting such "defeats" with a certain measure of equanimity, although the reaction to the vote on China's seat in the United Nations reminds us sharply that it is still a very precarious thing where a public defeat involves national pride and popular emotions. It may be that the Monroe Doctrine has finally lost its power to stir the *amour propre* of Americans and their Congress, but it is a certain thing that we are not yet at the point where the resurrection of such sentiments could be classed as a miracle. In fine, the O.A.S. arena is probably the most dangerous place that could be chosen for testing the

attachment of Americans to a Canada manifestly independent of the United States.

Parenthetically, it might be noted that while Canada has
generally regarded multilateral international agencies, notably
the U.N. and NATO, as providing a kind of "safety-in-
numbers" against United States domination, the composition
of the O.A.S., and especially the *sui generis* position of the
United States in hemispheric affairs, preclude any reliance by
Canada on such a rationale in this situation.

A disagreement between Canada and the United States at
the 1973 annual meeting of the Inter-American Development
Bank made clear that the possibility of confrontations in
hemispheric organizations is not idle speculation. As reported
in the *Financial Post* of Toronto:

> What Canada did at the Jamaica meeting was to stand
> up in the full glare of all attending governors and declare,
> in effect, that the bank should not be used as a lever and a
> whip to punish recipient countries involved in "bilateral"
> disputes over expropriation and compensation.
>
> The Canadian position . . . visibly angered U.S. Secretary
> of Treasury George Schultz. In his reply, Schultz made it
> clear that he thought Canada was wrong, and the U.S.
> would not change its determination to veto bank loans to
> Latin American countries that did not provide adequate
> compensation for expropriated U.S. properties. . . .
>
> This signals a fundamental and basic disagreement
> between the U.S. and Canada over bank policy. . . .
> Canada is in a tight squeeze between the U.S. and the
> Latin American member countries.[7]

The potential seriousness of such confrontations is evident.
The United States Treasury, the "heavy" in recent United
States-Canada difficulties, is often involved. It is an especially
delicate matter when, as in Inter-American Bank loans, over 80
percent of the money comes from the United States, and

Congress requires the United States to veto loans for countries failing to provide adequate compensation for expropriated United States properties.

How might the Canada-United States relationship have fared if Canada had borne full O.A.S. responsibilities at the time of the Bay of Pigs, the Dominican intervention, the acute disputes with Ecuador and Peru over high-seas fishing, and with Chile, and perhaps others, over expropriation issues and alleged political interference in the internal affairs of a nation? In the more distant future lies the possibility that U.S.-Canada issues which up to now have been solely bilateral may become charged with an O.A.S. interest and concern. With Canada a full member of the O.A.S., the organization's hemispheric jurisdiction could hardly be confined exclusively to problems and disputes under the aegis of the Southern Cross. Would such a development serve the United States-Canada relationship well?

It is, of course, possible that both Canada and the United States are ready to bet their high stakes in a healthy relationship with each other on a substantially more integrated hemisphere, and a Canada whose independence from the United States would increasingly be manifested in hemispheric affairs. Such a step might have a potential for long-run good, provided the run is long enough. One can only be sure that it is a bet that should not be pressed further by the United States without a genuinely searching scrutiny of the risk that two major American national interests could become disastrously crossgrained with each other. The potential for both added troubles in the relationship and new recriminations in the hemisphere is very great. Few exercises could produce more valuable insights into the realities and requirements of the United States national interest in an independent Canada than a rigourous reexamination of American policy on this matter.

Notes

1. John MacCormac, *Canada—America's Problem* (1940), pp. 32, 81.
2. *The Globe and Mail*, Toronto, February 7, 1972.

3. *The Ottawa Citizen*, February 8, 1972.

4. John Plank, Comments paper, Conference on Canada-United States Relations, Wingspread, 1969.

5. *Documents on American Foreign Relations—1961*, R. P. Stebbins, Editor (New York: Council on Foreign Relations), pp. 272-79.

6. J.C. M. Ogelsby, "Canada and the Pan American Union: Twenty Years on." 24 *International Journal*, 1969, pp. 571, 589, citing a 1967 paper by R. Craig Brown.

7. *The Financial Post*, Toronto, June 9, 1973.

CHAPTER 11

The "Special Relationship": Concept and Prospect

The "specialness" of the United States-Canada relationship until the early 1970s has been a staple in both fact and folklore. This specialness, while rooted in geography and history, has also been manifested in the unimpeded (until recently) intermingling of peoples, in American policies that well-intentioned Americans are unable to regard as really foreign and which equally well-intentioned Canadians have perceived as merely fitful elephantine slumber, in the unparalleled cultural and commercial integration of two national societies, and of course, in a border that has been more "undefended" in (and from) transnational rhetoric than any other boundary in human experience.

The rhetoric of "specialness" has itself often played a significant role—in illuminating, sometimes in masking—the realities against which national interests and policies are shaped and reshaped. In the post-World War II era the concept of a special relationship found concrete expression as policy in various areas, notable instances being the peacetime alliance exemplified in the North American Air Defense Command (NORAD) and the Defense Production Sharing arrangements, the exemption of Canada at Canada's request from United States restrictions on the outflow of United States capital in the 1960s, and the 1965 Automotive Agreement providing for free trade between the automobile industries of the two countries.

The zenith of special-relationship rhetoric was reached in the mid-1960s with an effort to give the concept greater functional significance under the rubric of "partnership." It was a venturesome, unprecedented step that President Johnson and Prime Minister Pearson took when they, as stated in a White House release, "in their first working meeting in Washington in January 1964 . . . agreed on the need for study of the basic principles of relations betweeen the United States and Canada." The seriousness with which this endeavor was undertaken is attested by the fact that both the President and the Prime Minister appointed to the task perhaps their most outstanding diplomatists in this field, Livingston T. Merchant and A. D. P. Heeney. Both men had twice headed embassies in Ottawa and Washington, and both brought to their assignment a broad knowledge of international affairs to match their intimate familiarity with the relationship. In short, if such an enterprise was ever to command promising sponsorship and adequate resources, this one did. And 1964 appeared to the President and the Prime Minister like a promising moment; it was, in fact, a singularly unpropitious time for such a bold venture.

Full-scale escalation of the Vietnam war stood in the wings, waiting to come on stage with its entourage of endless domestic and foreign complications for the United States. Both nations faced deepening internal crises: Canada with French-Canadian separatism, the United States with racial strife; the worldwide resurgence of nationalism fitted the mood of a Canada increasingly preoccupied with the interlocking problems of national identity and a ubiquitous American presence. And America's "national image" was beginning to lose its luster. In retrospect, it is hard to imagine how a more unpromising stage could have been set for a self-conscious Canada and an expanding American presence to play mutually supporting roles based on a script entitled "Principles for Partnership," featuring themes of "integration," "mutual involvement," "interdependence," "consultation," and "quiet diplomacy."

Yet there were favorable factors which led many to misread the portent of the 1964 heavens. The period from 1939 to 1964 had probably been the most harmonious twenty-five years in the history of the two countries. World War II had drawn them closer together in private activity and public policy than anyone, except perhaps the early American annexationists, had ever dared dream. Then came the Cold War with what seemed to be the first external security threat to North America in modern times. It was perceived in both countries as a common danger which could be countered only by close military collaboration. The NORAD continental-air-defense arrangements of 1957-58 bound the security of the United States and Canada together as never before, except in war. This alliance, more than any other single factor, encouraged Americans to assume that a continental, or North American, approach to the national interests of the two countries was a desirable and shared objective.

Partnership, as a rhetorical concept, had been embraced by both President Eisenhower and Prime Minister St. Laurent; on Eisenhower's visit with the Canadian leader in 1953, he foresaw the joint construction of the St. Lawrence Seaway as a manifestation of the "Canadian-American partnership." And when in 1961 President Kennedy advocated a United States-Canada partnership that would extend to inter-American affairs, the conceptual road to expanded collaboration was well established. Four years later, Lyndon Johnson and Lester Pearson were eager to consolidate and extend the era of collaboration.

Ambassadors Merchant and Heeney were quite aware that "Principles for Partnership" was reaching out for a more meaningful definition of the special relationship, certainly one that went beyond the hackneyed terminology of trading partners and other empty usages of the words partner and partnership. In urging the two nations, "actively to seek strengthening of the partnership," their Report, while noting continental defense as a major area where a structured, functioning partnership already existed, cautiously avoided any proposals for new structural arrangements. Instead, the emphasis was on developing existing consultative practices within a conceptual framework of partnership in order to advance national interests more effectively and more harmoniously. Ironically but significantly, it was the Report's pursuit of harmony that produced the greatest discord in Canada.

Strangely enough, in view of the disfavor with which the concept of continental partnership is now viewed in Canada, especially in nationalistic circles, very few Canadians found fault with the idea itself. The academic-publicist, James Eayrs, with his customary acuity and independence, was one of the few who regarded the idea of Canadian-American partnership as a dangerous dalliance with realities. In the United States, to the very limited extent the Report was noticed, proposals for a strong partnership elicited a taken-for-granted approval not unlike that accorded motherhood.

The discordant reception in Canada, as Arnold Heeney replied to the critics, "related not to the report as a whole, but to one paragraph, the meaning of which . . . was widely misunderstood." The paragraph in question had counselled "quiet diplomacy" on the part of the two governments in settling their differences and difficulties. Critics viewed such counsel as an invitation to subservience or "satellite" status on the part of Canada, and they were not reassured by the Report's explicit recognition of the right of the press and private persons to engage in public criticism of the other country. In retrospect, it seems likely that the stormy reaction to quiet diplomacy was not so much a misunderstanding of a specific recommendation as a subsconsicous rejection of the partnership idea itself. Under the premises and obligations of a meaningful partnership, quiet diplomacy would be a normal procedure for resolving differences. Yet to Canadian nationalists, a commitment to quiet diplomacy could hardly appear to be the high road to greater national independence.

What was an oblique rejection in the mid-1960s is clear-cut today: partnership in any meaningful sense, except perhaps in precisely delineated areas of common concern such as continental defense, is basically unacceptable to Canadian nationalists as a conceptual framework for the contemporary relations of Canada and the United States. American rhetoric and policy in turn would do well to accept the fact that, temptingly attractive as it is for us to characterize any close relationship in this way, true partnership involves a degree of defined common interest, mutuality of obligation, and prescribed behavior that simply is not realistic at least at present as a comprehensive conceptual framework for these two sovereign nations.

When two nations are as differently situated as these are by reason of history and disparities of power and responsibilities (differences, incidentally, that Ambassadors Merchant and Heeney noted in their report), an embracing partnership is likely to be a very difficult reach for both. Add to this the well-nigh insurmountable obstacle of assigning a proud, increasingly self-conscious Canada the *de facto* role of permanent junior partner, and it is not surprising that what seemed to be a good idea in 1964 seems now to be an idea whose time had not come.

In these circumstances the rhetoric of partnership ("continentalism," a term widely used pejoratively in Canada, little at all in the United States, "North Americanism" and "integration") has provided the miltiant nationalists with an attractive target. In fact, "partnership," except as a sparingly used throw-away term, has virtually disappeared from Canadian governmental usage even where as in continental defense arrangements it is genuinely meaningful.

The weather change is unmistakable in the conceptual rhetoric of the 1971 White Paper, *Defence in the 70s*, where, unlike in earlier defense documents, the word "partnership" makes no appearance. Although the view is still maintained that "in the defence of North America, Canada is inevitably closely associated with the United States," the association is now always characterized as "cooperation." Indeed cooperation is now perceived as "vital for sovereignty and security." "Independence," "sovereignty," and "independent political entity" now permeate the rhetoric. In this respect the defense White Paper of 1971 significantly follows the lead given by the foreign policy White Paper of 1970. What was both said and

left unsaid in that major review of foreign affairs made clear
the dramatic turnaround between the assertion of the Secretary of State for External Affairs in 1965 that "the conception
of partnership is central to our relations," and the ideas current only five years later.

The most authoritative view of the differences between
1965 and today in the Canadian perception of the relationship
is provided in Mitchell Sharp's 1972 exposition, *Canada-U.S.
Relations: Options for the Future*. One need hardly note the
omission of any reference to Merchant and Heeney's *Principles for Partnership*, which was laid to rest without being
mentioned at its own funeral, to be aware that important as
the United States relationship remains for Canada, its
"specialness" is no longer either taken for granted or, indeed,
regarded as a good thing.

Mr. Sharp suggested that on the American side the special
relationship is increasingly regarded as "an unbalanced relationship that . . . involved accommodations in favor of Canada
that are no longer tenable in the light of current economic and
political realities," while "on the Canadian side, there is a
concurrent feeling that special arrangements with the United
States . . . may in the end have curtailed our freedom of action
. . . and that the cumulative impact of such arrangements
taken together carries the risk of locking Canada more firmly
into a pattern of continental dependence."

Future realities may well require more of a special relationship than is now foreseen or desired in either country, but
today's climate is decidedly cool to the idea. In the foreseeable
future no Secretary of State for External Affairs is likely to be
tempted to reiterate the assertion of his predecessor in 1965
that "the conception of partnership is central to our relations"
with the United States.

The current United States negotiating stance toward Canada is more overtly nationalistic than it has been for some
decades. As Mr. Sharp suggested, with overtones of diplomacy's euphemisms, the United States is seeking "much
more demonstrable equity of benefit" between the countries.
But it is significant that American perception of the relationship has not changed nearly as much as the Canadian. In 1972

President Nixon found it easy and natural to reiterate Kennedy's portrayal of the relationship as a partnership. The same geopolitical and psychological factors that make Canadians wary of partnership operate in reverse on Americans, making it still seem an attractive concept for accommodating both a large American presence and Canadian independence.

Whether urged on Parliament by Presidents, expressed by a senior American diplomat in a recent Canadian press interview ("we think of our relationship with Canada in terms of partnership"), or manifested by American college students in their puzzled reaction on discovering the Merchant-Heeney Report is not gospel in Canada today ("what's wrong with partnership?"), the idea continues to be a deeply rooted, almost instinctive American response.

American attachment to partnership with Canada is also partly a byproduct of efforts to develop more satisfactory relations with an increasingly integrated Europe. The late unlamented figure of speech, "the dumbbell," to characterize European-American relations, created uneasiness in Canada that her interests would be ignored. To assuage this concern American officials have occasionally resorted to the idea of partnership with the United States as a way of including Canada, but Canadians remain uneasy about where "Canada fits into the developing pattern." As Minister Sharp put it in May 1973, following Dr. Kissinger's Atlantic Charter address, "We don't want to be polarized around any of the main power centres."

In this as elsewhere Canada now leaves no doubt about wanting to be more independent of the United States relationship, rejecting "closer integration" (Option Two) as well as the status quo (Option One) in favor of Option Three's "comprehensive strategy" aimed at "greater Canadian distinctiveness" and trade diversification. And yet within the decade developments elsewhere could conceivably make greater North American economic integration attractive, perhaps even a virtual necessity. Keeping the future open for a positive response to this possibility should be a prudent concern of United States policy. Today's nationalism largely bars Canada from doing so. In a May 1973 comment on Canada's options, Mitchell Sharp was unequivocal: "Economic integration with the United States as a direction of policy we ruled out as unacceptable to the Canadian people."

The United States cannot challenge this judgment. Neither, however, need it accept Canada's current mood as foreclosing a future that may require more regional collaboration. It is not necessary that United States policy postulate such a future, but keeping it open as a viable alternative will require two things: first, that the United States take seriously Canada's concerns about independent nationhood, thereby helping to allay them, and second, that United States policy not reciprocate Canada's nationalism with tit-for-tat responses. Whether American nationalism is sufficiently mature to bear the burdens of such understanding and restraint will depend on statesmanship in both the private and public sectors of American life.

Canadian leadership is not unmindful that in seeking less vulnerability, there is a risk of missing opportunities for creative collaboration. Mr. Sharp's policy prospectus devotes its six closing paragrpahs to demonstrating that there can be no thought of disturbing the harmony of the relationship. Indeed, he may have protested a little too much in saying that "all these options have one common demoninator: the need for the relationship to be harmonious. . . . There is nothing in all this that should be thought to imply a scenario for greater contention. Far from it."

Canada's search for a new strategy in her international affairs will take time to prove itself, and inevitably this will also be a testing time for the durability of the American commitment to an independent Canada. If a strategy emphasizing greater national distinctiveness and more international diversity is the way to a more confident Canada and a more mature relationship, the United States should respond with a positive attitude.

If, on the other hand, the international community, particularly the E.E.C., develops in ways that make regionalism the "wave of the future," the ability of the United States and Canada to meet the challenge will depend on a Canada more confident than she is today that closer economic integration is compatible with her independent nationhood, and a United States able and willing to respond positively (but not dominate) in fashioning a more collaborative relationship. Both will require the teaching of experience.

If unhappily the European community should lose its will for unity, an alternative projected as a realistic possibility in 1974 by Theodore Geiger of the National Planning Association, the likely resurgence of American hegemony in the affairs of the West might well enhance the importance of Canada of closer economic relations with the United States. This is not to say that Canada faces nothing but a Hobson's choice. It does, however, suggest that, paradoxically, the deeply rooted integrative forces with the United States would likely be strengthened rather than weakened by major negative developments elsewhere in the world.

Happily for the American interest, nothing so unrealistic as mortgaging present policies to an unforeseen future is involved. Several fundamental policy considerations are as pertinent for the health of today's relationship as they are imperative to a prudent concern for the future.

First is American self-restraint. At this point, major policy initiatives are generally better left to Canada, if for no other reason than that they are usually perceived by Canadians to be far more critical to Canada than to the United States. What may be a give-or-take policy problem for the United States often assumes the proportions of a nationhood concern in Canada. Time and circumstances may moderate the need for American restraint, but for the foreseeable future Americans would do well to assume that the Subcommittee on Foreign Economic Policy of the United States House of Representatives spoke perceptively in 1972 in observing that "all [Canadians] want to avoid a policy which is simply submissive to or derived from U.S. policy."

As for rhetorical initiatives, such as visions of an embracing "partnership" of the two nations, while the time may conceivably come when Canadians will again readily proclaim that the "conception of partnership is central to our relations," the last thing today's situation calls for is unrequited avowals of partnership advanced by the United States, primarily to make the geopolitical disparities of the relationship more acceptable. Such euphemisms do a disservice to a more realistic and sensitive understanding on the part of Americans and fuel rather than allay Canadian apprehensions. A second consideration is even more fundamental. If Ambassadors Merchant and Heeney misjudged the Canadian mood in their espousal of partnership and quiet diplomacy, they surely were on target in another respect. Ambassador Heeney told his critics that the Report's "consistent aim, and . . . central recommendation . . . [is] the establishment and maintenance of a regime of . . . 'intimate, timely, and continuing consultation,' a regime in which Canada can—when and where it counts—bring to bear effective influence upon United States attitudes and policies." As events have often confirmed, "effective consultation" is where the specialness of the relationship is either won or lost.

There are great possibilities for strain and disappointment in a special relationship, as many nations can attest, but nothing is resented quite so much as the unfulfilled expectation of being consulted. Speed and secrecy are traditional enemies of consultation, and when they are used to carry out nationalistic ventures, consultation usually becomes mere notification, with little or no lead time over the headlines. Such was the case wih Canada's unilateral assertion of jurisdiction over coastal and Arctic seas in 1971, Washington's imposition of a 10-percent surcharge on imports in the same year, and the Canadian export tax on oil in 1973, although in the latter instance there was a little more lead time in the notification.

Ambassadors Merchant and Heeney accepted the reality that on occasion the processes of consultation would be overridden; their antidote for limiting such exigencies was that "the judgment in such circumstances should be that of the highest authority." Yet the higher the decision to bypass consultation, the more grievous the blow to the relationship. Whatever the level on which the decision is taken not to consult, the relationship clearly cannot withstand many such instances. Trust and confidence between governments are grounded in effective consultation, a subject that merits greater analytical and creative attention than it has received.

Although the Merchant-Heeney Report was able to list ten "Joint United States-Canada Entities," along with dozens of American federal and state agencies which deal directly with their Canadian counterparts, few of them serve as systematic, sustained means for effective consultation. Aside from the joint-command arrangements of NORAD, and the notable work of the International Joint Commission which has dealt primarily with boundary waters and most recently with pollution problems, there have been few joint agencies charged with broad consultation responsibilities. Joint cabinet-level committees have either languished or functioned with a spasmodic, wasting symbolic usefulness that does not suggest a great unrealized potential for such ventures.

The Canada-United States Interparliamentary Group, launched in 1959, provides a useful forum for the exchange of views between individual members of Congress and Parliament. Its potential, however, is generally judged by students and participants alike to be greater than its achievement. A recent study of the group's experience modestly concluded that it "fulfils the requirements for continued existence"; and yet, a prominent Canadian participant, Senator M. Gratton O'Leary, writing the study's Foreword, views the enterprise as "a vision fading; a way being lost." And Mathew Abrams, its author, observed that "official sources tend to praise the strengthened bonds of North American partnership . . . arising from the Group's deliberations," but candidly recognized that "others . . . suggest that the whole structure of Canadian-American cooperation is ramshackle and inadequate and that the Group is representative of the 'patchwork of committees which meets now and then about this and that.' " [2]

The reason for the limited development of systematic consultation is that neither government has encouraged it. Both have preferred to rely mainly on the ad hoc processes of traditional diplomacy, supplemented by direct dealing between functional departments of the two governments, and to some extent between states and provinces. This has resulted in a make-do type of decentralized consultation that at times defies coordination by the foreign offices. The oft-repeated litany of professional diplomacy, reiterated by Ambassadors

Merchant and Heeney, is that more willingness rather than more apparatus is all that is necessary. That is a view of the matter whose time has almost certainly passed.

Conventional caution is rightly wary of encumbering human problems with mindless machinery. This wariness plus a concern that functional consultation agencies may impair national sovereignty, not to speak of the prerogatives of diplomacy, mean that such arrangements get more critical than creative attention. This caution has reflected two paradoxical concerns: Canada fears such agencies would be dominated by the United States; the United States fears they would complicate and impede its freedom of action within as well as outside the relationship. Neither country is ready to entrust matters of concern to large, new joint authorities. More effective consultation is presently the only realistic aspiration.

Even consultation arrangements will have to be developed selectively, in areas where tomorrow's big problems and opportunities will require more sustained, more systematic, more sophisticated attention than traditional diplomacy can hope to maintain. Let it be quickly added that this is not to suggest that meaningful consultation and the ongoing adjustment of policies can be carried on without the help of the diplomatic process; it is simply to say that in such areas as energy, conservation of resourcs, trade, and finance, including their interacting inflations, these two advanced societies will increasingly require more consultation and collaboration than is possible through existing ad-hoc processes. The form and responsibilities of such oversight would, of course, vary with the subject, but short of having any power of decision (unless specifically authorized as with certain aspects of the International Joint Commission), the basic function would be to monitor and evaluate designated transnational activities. Emerging problems could be identified before they become crises, and appropriate courses of action could be recommended.

For example, as suggested earlier, the need of the two nations to develop effective collaboration in the conservation of energy may be a particularly promising opportunity. It might also be feasible to create a joint agency, perhaps composed of both official and private persons, to monitor and evaluate the experience with the free trade in the automotive equipment provided for in the 1965 Auto Pact. The 1971-72 cabinet-level troubles over the pact would seem to point in that direction in order to assist in resolving difficulties before they involve domestic political positions and national prestige. Indeed, this particular contretemps may well be an instructive near miss in the damage that could result if the fine-tuning of trade policy in major areas is left primarily to the vagaries of cabinet-level diplomacy and politics. Another possible area for such joint oversight is the defense-production-sharing arrangement with its changing problems as it comes increasingly under the influence of new industrial policies in both countries.

Canada and the United States have had a good experience with institutionalizing their consultative processes in two important instances—the International Joint Commission (I.J.C.) and, less significantly perhaps, the Permanent Joint Defense Board (P.J.B.D.). It is entirely possible that the selective extension of such joint ventures would help both nations deal constructively with the potentially self-destructive concerns of their mounting nationalisms. At the same time, more effective consultation processes would provide the one element of specialness in the relationship in which all collaborative policies, whatever the subject, must be rooted.

The readiness to give creative attention to this strategic hedge against inwardly oriented preoccupations is yet to be tested. Both countries have special difficulties to surmount. On the United States side is the inescapable fact that there are many claimants to consultation. It is increasingly evident that the United States may already be overextended in this respect, unable to meet the expectations of its friends, allies, and neighors. Taking realistic account of the worldwide responsibilities of the nation, and especially the limitations of international consultations imposed by internal processes, the United States may now be much more seriously out of balance in its inability to fulfill these expectations than it is with respect to its substantive commitments. In some matters, however, institutional arrangements could actually reduce the demands on today's overloaded ad hoc processes.

On the Canadian side, the current preoccupation is with the

dilemma of how much of what kind of specialness it needs and wants. How much is necessary for Canada's viability as a modern industrial society and how much is too much for the good health of an independent Canada? The Trudeau Government, speaking through both Mitchell Sharp and his successor, Allan J. MacEachen as Secretary of State for External Affairs, has been explicit in pronouncing an end to a special relationship based on more special policy arrangements with the United States. On the other hand, neither minister suggested that Canada would be cool toward developing more effective consultation processes. To the contrary, Mr. MacEachen in his first major statement on relations with the United States laid special emphasis on the need for more effective consultation, going so far as to say: "I want to conclude with a strong plea for the merits of the consultative approach. For Canada it is, after all, the only sensible way to conduct business with the U.S." [3]

Canada may, however, often prefer multilateral rather than bilateral forums for consultation. In the past she has tended to be wary of joint agencies lest they be dominated by the United States, but if, as experience seems to suggest, agencies with balanced representation can help keep bilateral policy problems from escalating into cabinet-level controversies, Canada may discover even more genuine independence in these arrangements than in traditional diplomacy. High-level diplomatic confrontations almost invariably bring into play a preponderance of United States power.

Assuming the United States remains committed to the maintenance of effective Canadian independence as an American national interest, it should not fear the consequences of a strong positive stance on consultative arrangements. Indeed, it is the one area today where meaningful initiatives could be peculiarly the prerogative of the more powerful nation.

Above and beyond the realm of foreign policy and diplomacy, there is a growing transnational reality of specialness that transcends public policies. In a social science perspective the totality of the relationship is gradually acquiring an organic integrity of its own which, being unorganized and unrecognized, over the long pull may moderate the temper of nationalistic sentiments and the policies of the governments.

This "third-dimensional" aspect is far more deeply embedded but far less articulated than the "continentalism" feared by Canada's nationalists and now shunned by its reponsible spokesmen. It is a phenomenon that has begun to attract the interest of social scientists. In its spreading web of seamless activity, even the democratic processes of these two societies are not as separable as classical international relations and diplomacy have assumed. To cite only several examples: the intermingling of legislators in the Canada-United States Interparliamentary Group, the frequent appearance of American and Canadian witnesses before tribunals in the other nation, and the spectacle of striking Canadian unionists picketing a company in California. There are also such popular manifestations as the receipt in Washington of upward to five thousand Canadian communications a week in the fall of 1971, protesting the projected nuclear test at Amchitka.

It is a good bet that the insulating authority of this international border will increasingly be diffused by the osmotic forces of participatory democracy. Such developments generate their own dimension of specialness, a dimension which in the long run will probably prove more difficult for governments to constrain than the behavior of multinational corporations. The proliferation of transnational activities, while having no kinship with a contrived "continentalism" that would amalgamate the two nations, is nonetheless a clear manifestation of an indigenous continentalism that geographically, historically, and ubiquitously daily binds the nations together in a relationship very unlike holy matrimony but nonetheless "for better for worse."

Both nations will, of course, exert their own influence on how the balance between better and worse is struck. For the foreseeable future, Canadian actions with a nationalistic orientation will likely be to the fore, and the United States may be doing most of the reacting. And yet, the main impulse behind Canadian nationalism being the American presence in its many forms, the balance cannot help but be powerfully influenced by "the American fact."

The life force of the United States-Canada relationship
flows from its unique potential for the symbiosis of "intimate
living together of two dissimilar organisms in a mutually beneficial relationship." In a time of both resurgent nationalism
and unprecedented interdependence, extraordinary levels of
statecraft and public understanding are required to foster
processes and policies that respond to exigencies without
foreclosing future opportunities.

Diplomacy will long continue front and center in the official
relations of the two nations. Even though private attitudes
and activities are the dominant dynamics of the relationship,
the governments must be mindful that on both sides of the
border the citizenry are susceptible to negative leads from
officialdom.

Basically perhaps the most taken-for-granted and least appreciated specialness of the United States-Canada relationship is the fact that its energies need not be negatively
oriented toward averting disaster or merely achieving the
tolerable; with all its difficulties, it is probably the only international relationship where optimum collaboration is potentially a realistic aspiration. If that potential is to be pursued in
both collaboration and national independence, ad hoc diplomacy, good as it generally has been, will increasingly need
to be supplemented by ongoing joint agencies. Such structures
of process in support of enlightened national policies will only
be acceptable and effective when designed for specific functional purposes and not as loosely conceived omnibus mech-
anisms. Their main service would be more systematic consultation, better-digested information, and more maturely
formulated recommendations. In a few closely defined areas,
there may be opportunities in the future for joint agencies
with more authority. Whatever the designated jurisdiction
and delegated duties, the basic organizational principle will
assuredly have to be balanced national representation.

Systematic consultation as the next step in a more
rewarding collaborative process, like better public understanding, is no longer merely a nicety to be sought when other
more pressing problems permit; in reality it is today the only
policy thrust sufficiently fundamental to reach and head off

the endemic mischief that nationalistic excesses may otherwise introduce into the policies of both countries.

And beyond the continuing fire-brigade work of extinguishing nationalistic brush fires and preventing conflagrations, there will be the increasingly outsized tasks of modern statecraft in guilding the development of the relationship as an international community already burgeoning with a life of its own while still the possessed creature of two independent national societies.

Canadian nationalism, in the best positive sense, is now rooted in a national experience of its own. Nevertheless, it cannot soon be fully free of a reactive preoccupation with the ubiquitous American presence. The level of this negative concern will vary inversely with the confidence of Canadians in the reality of their independence, and nothing outside Canada will bear more decisively on this than the ability or inability of American nationalism to see and deal with this reality as part of the American national interest.

The climate for creative venturing in statecraft is rarely beckoning, but both countries—certainly Canada no less than the United States—have a stake in not permitting the concept of a genuinely independent Canada as a realistic American national interest to languish in the dustbins of idle rhetoric. Sustained collaboration through both improved understanding and better processes is the *sine qua non* of higher ceilings for tomorrow's policies and perhaps of an optimum relationship the day after tomorrow. Indeed, even today's problem-clouded weather could hardly fail to benefit.

Notes

1. *Looking Ahead*, the National Planning Association, Vol. 22, No. 1 (February 1974).
2. *The Canada-United States Interparliamentary Group*, by Mathew J. Abrams (Ottawa: Parliamentary Centre for Foreign Affairs and Foreign Trade; and Toronto: Canadian Institute for International Affairs, 1973, pp. v, vii.
3. Address in Winnipeg, Manitoba, January 23, 1975, reported in *Canada Weekly*, Department of External Affairs, February 5, 1975.

Index

197